The School Leader

Surviving and Thriving

Become more effective, efficient, and confident in your role as a school leader. This book provides tips, strategies, and inspirational stories to help you overcome common challenges, improve school culture, make deeper connections with parents and staff, and more. Appropriate for K–12 leaders in any type of setting, this updated edition includes new tips on handling difficult situations and being a connected educator. Each chapter presents key tips in quick, concise chunks so that you can easily implement one strategy at a time and survive and thrive in your leadership role. Take these tips and make them your own, so you can do your best for your students and staff!

Andrew Marotta is Principal at Port Jervis High School in Port Jervis, New York, where he has been a leader for 16 years, first serving as Assistant Principal and then Principal. He also hosts the Education Leadership and Beyond Podcast #ELB and authors the weekly #ELBlog. Follow him on Twitter @andrewmarotta21.

The School Leader

Surviving and Thriving

144 Points of Wisdom, Practical Tips, and Relatable Stories

2nd Edition

Andrew Marotta

Routledge
Taylor & Francis Group

NEW YORK AND LONDON

Second edition published 2021
by Routledge
52 Vanderbilt Avenue, New York, NY 10017

and by Routledge
2 Park Square, Milton Park, Abingdon, Oxon, OX14 4RN

*Routledge is an imprint of the Taylor & Francis Group,
an informa business*

First edition published by Andrew Marotta 2017

Library of Congress Cataloging-in-Publication Data
Names: Marotta, Andrew, author.
Title: The school leader surviving and thriving : 144 points of
    wisdom, practical tips, and relatable stories / Andrew Marotta.
Description: Second edition. | New York, NY : Routledge, 2021. |
    Includes bibliographical references.
Identifiers: LCCN 2020041165 (print) | LCCN 2020041166 (ebook) |
    ISBN 9780367422615 (hardback) | ISBN 9780367421717
    (paperback) | ISBN 9780367823009 (ebook)
Subjects: LCSH: School principals. | Educational leadership.
Classification: LCC LB2831.9 .M355 2021 (print) | LCC LB2831.9
    (ebook) | DDC 371.2/012—dc23
LC record available at https://lccn.loc.gov/2020041165
LC ebook record available at https://lccn.loc.gov/2020041166

ISBN: 978-0-367-42261-5 (hbk)
ISBN: 978-0-367-42171-7 (pbk)
ISBN: 978-0-367-82300-9 (ebk)

Typeset in Palatino
by Apex CoVantage, LLC

Contents

3 School Stuff: Connect With the Kids and Create a Super Dope Culture

Acknowledgments

This project has been an amazing experience. I love what I do as a principal and educator, and this book is an extension of my work in those roles. I also very much love my family, and would like to thank them for supporting me throughout this endeavor. My beautiful wife, Jennifer, and my three awesome children, Claire, Matthew, and Tessa, have given me encouragement, ideas, suggestions, and most importantly, the time. I could not have completed this book without them believing in me. I heard a great quote recently that we will adopt as a family motto: "In this family, love is spelled: t.i.m.e." I thank my amazing family for the time they have given me to write this book. I'd also like to thank my mother and father, Dorothy and Joseph Marotta. My dad passed almost nine years ago now, but the lessons and drive that my parents taught me live on in my values as a parent and a professional. My mom continues to be my biggest fan, not only as her son, but also in my work as a principal and a basketball official. I can't thank her enough for her unwavering support behind all my goals and endeavors.

I would also like to thank my siblings, Suzanne, Maureen, and Paul, as well as my in-laws, the Grimes family: Patricia and Eugene Grimes, Kelly and Ron Bentley, and Susan and Rich Bila. My family has provided great encouragement. They have given helpful, wise feedback to keep A-Lotta Marotta in check. I thank them for their love.

To my mentors who have hired me, guided me, and molded me over the last 12 years: John Xanthis, John Bell, Tony DiMarco, and Tom Bongiovi. These men have spent time and energy to share their wisdom and experience with me. They appear time and again throughout this book, in specific stories of how they have helped me. I am forever grateful for my relationships with these fine educators and gentlemen.

To all of the teachers, counselors, and staff at Port Jervis High School, especially my secretary, Reenie Nicolette, and my assistant principals Heidi Nyland, Tom Rickard, and formerly Jared Kahmar, who has now gone on to be principal of another school: I thank all of you immensely for allowing me the privilege of being your leader. You have all put up with me and assisted me along the way. We have learned from one another and done good work for our students. I respect the work you do for our students and community.

To Dr. Rob Gilbert, sports psychologist and teacher at Montclair State University in New Jersey. It was Dr. Gilbert's urging and inspiration that pushed me to put pen to paper, or fingers on the keyboard. He made me believe that I could write this book and mapped it out for me. His words of encouragement and his daily success hotline (call 973–743–4690) have been priceless. Dr. Gilbert truly is changing the world one student at a time.

I've learned many lessons from my parents, my work as principal, as a husband and parent myself, and also through my work as a college basketball official. Enforcing the rules on the court in high-pressure situations, with rambunctious fans and talented coaches and players in a fast-moving game, offers surprising comparisons to my job as principal. Oddly enough, they are very similar. I have to make quick decisions with poise using my knowledge and experience of the game, my gut, and the rule book. I am charged to be respectful in my duties and firm in my convictions, all while under a bright light and intense scrutiny. I want to thank my referee supervisors: John Clougherty, Bryan Kersey, and Reggie Greenwood. These men all have successful officiating careers as well as professional and personal lives. It is a fine balancing act, and I thank them for the opportunities they have given me, along with the experiences they have shared and lessons they have taught me. They are strong men and great leaders who have helped steer me to this point.

Finally, to the many, many students and families I have met and served over the years, it is my hope that I have treated you with grace and respect. Whether we agreed or disagreed on a singular issue, it was always my intention to treat you fairly and with integrity.

Introduction: Make It Happen

You are going to read that throughout this book. I write this phrase often purposefully, because you are the leader. You are in charge and if it is to be, it is up to you. So very simply put, make it happen. That is my charge to you. You bought this book for a reason. What was it? You felt like spending money? You bought this book because you want to get better. You want to add some things to your repertoire to improve on your daily practice as principal. So . . . make it happen. Don't wait until September. Don't wait until winter break. Do it now. Today.

In addition, not every one of these points might be for you. Pick the ones you really like and make them your own. Tweak them, change them, and add to them. I didn't reinvent the wheel here, just put together some practical ideas that I believe can help you become a better principal—whether you have been at this for 20 years or you are starting this September. Maybe you used to do some of these tips or practices and you got away from it. Maybe you are accepting your first principal-ship and you are going to implement all of these! I love it and get after it.

Thank you for buying my book, and I hope that you enjoy it. I hope you implement change and improve your practices. I hope you impact the hearts and minds of your students, and I hope you are making the world a better place by being a great principal!

Enjoy . . .

Introduction to the New Edition: The Power of a Single Experience

Who knew that the power of one single experience could change the course of your life? That's what happened and that's what I'm hoping could happen to you after reading this book. In the fall of 2016, I visited Dr. Rob Gilbert's graduate education leadership class at Montclair State University located in New Jersey. I talked leadership, I talked education, and I talked officiating college basketball. Dr. Gilbert and I hit it off immediately. He and the class enjoyed the presentation. And there was great energy all around. As I left, Dr. Gilbert handed me 10 books, and two of them were his. He said to me, "Where is your book Andrew?" I laughed and said "Doc, there's no way. I have three kids, I am a high school principal, a college basketball official, and just don't have the time." He pressed on saying, "You have to do it. You are a great principal and should share some of your techniques. You don't have to write the whole book, just write down the things you do as a principal." Well, being blessed with ADD, (it's a superpower, not a curse) that night I had 60 tips. The next day while at school using my notepad, I wrote down at least 40 more, so in less than 24 hours I had 100 tips found in this book.

The Power of a Single Experience

Because Dr. Rob Gilbert believed in me and challenged me and saw something in me that I did not see in myself, that prompt, that experience, changed my life.

So here we are almost 5 years later at the release of *The Principal Surviving and Thriving*, now named *The School Leader Surviving and Thriving*. So much has changed. I have stepped away from officiating due to the overwhelming response from the book. I have shifted my focus to try to help make a positive impact on the lives of others. I realized quickly after doing my first few presentations and workshops that no matter how great a game I officiated, I was not having a positive impact on the lives of others. Now, whether it is through live or virtual workshops, podcasts, Leadership Sparks episodes, and so on, I can connect and positively influence the lives of so many school leaders and in turn, hopefully, help create more positive cultures and schools around the world. That's what this is all about. We as school leaders can have a tremendous impact on the lives of those we serve. It is my goal that this book can help you do that. Please refer to the guide on how to best implement the practices in this book. We are tasked with enriching the lives of others and making our schools the best they can be.

Pandemic, racial and social injustices, political unrest, (2020) whatever the scenario is, while our jobs might be changing due to all of these scenarios that have happened, the goal remains the same: to enrich and impact those lives in the best way we can. There are many helpful tips, tricks, and hacks in here to help you. Take these and make them your own. Implement them today, tomorrow, and in any time or place that you can. One tip at a time, one student at a time, one powerful experience at a time. Just like Dr. Rob Gilbert changed my life with the power of a single experience, you can do that for others. Find those moments, find those students, and find the sparks in them and help them out using these many techniques and strategies present in this book. Thank you for reading and my best to you. #KeepRolling. #SurviveThrive

Best,

Andrew Marotta
Educator, Author, Speaker, Professional
Developer, Leadership Professor, & former
NCAA Basketball Official

917-385-9430
"mail to: andrewmarottallc@gmail.com"
"https://twitter.com/@andrewmarotta21"
"http://www.andrewmarotta.com"

1

Be a Better Leader

1. Treat every kid as if they are your kid.

This is the golden rule of hiring people, and our daily philosophy with our staff. Love kids. Act it. Demonstrate it. Treat them the way you want your own children to be treated. This is the number one best thing you can do as principal, which is why this is the first wisdom point. You will read this theme in multiple tips and sections throughout the book.

It will make your job so much easier if you have people around you who adopt this way of working with students in the school. It doesn't mean be a pushover and give them anything they want. That's not loving kids, nor is it good parenting. Some of our best teachers are the toughest and run the most challenging classrooms, but they love the kids. Add compassion, understanding, forgiveness, kindness, openness, and humor. This winning combination reaches out and is felt by each student.

We actually listen for people to say that they love kids when we ask them why we should hire them over other candidates. It has been said that children are like dogs (not meant in a derogatory way!) in that they can sense a phony a mile away, and instinctively feel love in people with whom they interact. So hire people who love kids and listen for it in the interview. When the students feel love, they do better in school and have a better overall experience. If you create this type of environment in your school, you will never regret it.

2. Don't ignore small irritants. Meet them head on and address them on a daily basis. You're in charge.

Whether it is that same teacher coming in late, staff or students parking where they shouldn't, a door that squeaks all day long, or a custodian who does not clean their area well . . . don't ignore these things. The buck stops with you. If you allow these things to slide, so will everyone else. They are watching you and testing you all the time to see how you handle things. Don't let the little stuff go. When you see it, address it. If you cannot fix or manage it immediately, put it on your to-do list until it gets done. Make it happen. If you allow the small irritants to pile up, you will surely have a big mess.

As a young teen, I worked in my dad's pharmacy. We grew up in a nice area of Staten Island, NY, called Ward's Hill, near the ferry. The pharmacy was right near the docks in a not-so-hot neighborhood called Tompkinsville. My dad was one of many good people in that neighborhood who really cared and tried to keep it clean. Part of my job was to sweep the sidewalks each day and make sure the outside of the shop was spotless. If there was graffiti on the wall, I had to paint it right away.

One time there was a graffiti artist who would not quit. I'd paint the wall, and he'd be back the next night. I'd paint it again, and he'd be back again. I complained to my dad that we were just wasting time and money, and he'd calmly say to just go out there and paint it. "We will not let him win." My father would not be beat. This went on for about two weeks until, finally, I came in the next day and we had a clean wall. I was so proud. I felt like good had conquered evil when I beat that graffiti artist.

I learned a valuable lesson through that experience. Don't let small irritants go. The store might have been fine on the inside, but if we had left that graffiti there, it would have given us a poor image and sent the wrong message to the community. It would have shown neglect. That graffiti bothered my dad and he would not let it go. He took pride in his store and cared too much about the community to let vandalism win.

3. Show people that you care.

People do not care how much you know unless they know how much you care. This profession is all about connecting with people. You can be the smartest person, the best dresser, have the best teaching tools, and know the most about curriculum, but if your people believe that you don't care about them, you have no shot. You have to show that you care about the school, the kids, the staff, and the parents. You are the leader of a community, and you need to genuinely show interest in that community's well-being.

When someone is sick, ask about them. When someone dies, go to the services. When a staff member's former student gets accepted into college, wins an award, has a baby, and so on, acknowledge and celebrate those things. It is important to communicate through your actions that people matter to you. Be consistent. Use each child's name. Invest your heart and attention beyond the classroom, offices, and so on. Take a moment to show up. There is a famous line from the poet, Maya Angelou: "People will forget what you said, they will forget what you did, but they will never forget how you made them feel."

4. Don't be, look, or act defeated.

You are the leader. You are in charge. If you act positively, most (I repeat, most) will follow your lead. If you look or act defeated and overwhelmed, that is how your staff will respond and act with students. Even if you inevitably feel that you are in over your head sometimes, do not let it show. Snap out of it and look the part.

Think about when you go to a comedy show or any kind of entertainment venue. How about a wedding, or a concert? When that MC, DJ, or singer grabs the mic, you notice their body language right away. Whatever may be going on in their personal life or backstage, their energy affects the audience, and away they go with their show. Well, you have a show every day, and regardless of what is going on in your building, do not look or act defeated.

This is from my good buddy, Dr. Robert Gilbert, sports psychologist at Montclair State University, in NJ: "Your actions change your attitude, your motions change emotions, and your movements change your moods." Be positive at all times. Make it happen.

5. Beg, borrow, and steal ideas that work in other schools and use them in your building.

As I sit writing this section of the book, I am in a middle school in Pennsylvania, attending my daughter's swim meet. (She won her first-ever heat!) On my way in I saw a bench in the hallway named the Buddy bench. I love it and already took a picture of it and will be sending it to our tech department. I want it in our school!

John Xanthis, our former superintendent and now current Superintendent of Valley Central Schools in Montgomery, NY, gave me a great idea once, something he had done at one of his former schools: Free Coffee Fridays. A group of volunteer students delivers coffee to staff members on Friday afternoons, for free! I loved the idea and took it to use for my own staff. It was a big hit, and we still run it to this day. Take these ideas and make them your own; put them to work for you. Being a great leader doesn't have to mean reinventing the wheel. Pay attention to your peers, colleagues, and mentors. Learn great ideas from others and put them to work in your school.

6. Adopt a "Captain of the Ship" mentality.

A parent falls on a water spill in the auditorium. There is a fight between both teams at the boys' basketball game. The Board of Education member's child is caught cheating on a final exam needed for graduation. The ski club sneaks alcohol on the trip. These are all real events that can happen any and every day, and they are all your fault. Yes, they are. You may be asking yourself, How are these my fault? I wasn't even at the basketball game. . . . There is one simple answer that you must understand to do well as principal: You are the captain of the ship.

You are the principal, and everything that happens in and around your building is a reflection of and on you. If something happens on your watch, take responsibility. Use the words, "I am sorry this happened to you, and as the person in charge I take full responsibility." I learned this from my friend and mentor, Tom Bongiovi. (He likes to say he's related to the singer, but he's not.)

Tom had on his desk, as principal and later, as superintendent, "The buck stops here" sign from the days of President Harry S. Truman. I watched Mr. B and learned from him that it shows strength to accept ownership and invest in what you are doing and where you are. Do not blame the superintendent, the Board of Education, the teachers, the community, the custodians, and especially not the students. Do not blame the students. You are the boss and it falls on you. People will respect you for it.

Naturally, the goal is to make sure these things do not occur on your watch, but if they do, it is up to you to handle any situation appropriately. Acknowledge the issue or challenge and communicate transparently with all related parties to fix the problem or resolve the conflict. Make it happen.

7. Stay calm but don't be afraid to use a little extra mustard.

Lots happening: Snowstorm, fire alarm rings, and you have a three-car accident out in front of your school. You are in charge. Stay calm, boss. Everyone is following your lead.

They are watching you, wondering what you'll do and how you are going to manage this. Take a moment, catch your breath, and make smart decisions. This goes for a genuine emergency or any one of a hundred crises large and small that can and do happen on any given day: a parent is bashing you at a school board meeting, there is a heart attack in the faculty room, there is flooding in the girls' locker room, the list goes on. You will handle it and do so with confidence and skill. That's the principal's job.

So where is the mustard and what the heck does that mean? Well, this mustard has nothing to do with a hot dog. It has to do with you matching the intensity of the situation with your body language, tone, and energy to let people know you mean business. Like a Mustang cruising down the road revving its engine every once in a while, or a singer with a knockout voice hitting that amazing note, from time to time you need to remind people that you are there. So you put a lil' extra mustard in it. This might mean raising your voice to clear the hallway after a fight, or calling an emergency faculty meeting after school to address something important. Remind everyone that you are captain of the ship.

I recently went into a freshmen class, 8th period. There was a brand-new teacher in there; only his second day on the job. The students were being disrespectful, loud, and obnoxious. I was walking by and heard the noise from the room. I stopped in, stayed very calm, but let them know in a strong, stern voice that we were not going to have this. I didn't need a lot of mustard in that moment, but a little squeeze to send the message to those students that they needed to get in line. It is my hope that the teacher will follow my lead and take control of the situation. I will be following up with him and we shall see.

Another event that sticks with me from years back is one particular fire drill. It was seven degrees outside, and there was a false alarm that tripped the fire alarms. The building began to evacuate quickly. I said in my head Ohh sh*t! I knew we only had a few minutes before we had to do something.

The rule is that all students and staff stay outside until the local fire department arrives; but I knew on that freezing day that I could not have my people outside for ten minutes or more while we waited for the fire department, so I hustled to find out what had caused the alarm. It was a heat sensor in the cooking room. There was no fire, no emergency, and all was okay. That took me about 40 seconds to find out. I made an executive decision that we would bring the students and staff into the gym and auditorium until the fire department arrived and gave the green light. I put the order out over the walkie-talkies and they came inside.

The fire department eventually arrived, cut off the alarms and I was summoned to the custodial office. The fire chief was there, questioning why I brought my people back inside prior to his crew's arrival. I explained that with the outdoor temperatures, I had determined the alarm was not an emergency and decided to let the kids and staff back in. Well. Well. Well. That led to an epic tongue lashing from the chief, but I took most of it and eventually had to stand up for my decision with—you guessed it—a little mustard.

My final note on this is to stay calm no matter what, pick your battles carefully, and don't be shy about throwing in a little mustard when you need to.

8. Be the most energetic and enthusiastic person in the building.

This does not take any talent or skill, it is simply in your heart and mind: Be the most enthusiastic and energetic person in the building. I cannot stress enough how important this is. There are another 124 tips in this book, but this one is way up there with the most important of all: Get after it! Bring the energy each and every day. Your students will feed off it and your staff will, too.

If the principal's energy and enthusiasm fade, so does the school. Each and every one of you need to know, understand, and take this to heart—extra sleep, vitamin C, coffee, Mountain Dew, prayers . . . do whatever you have to do for energy when you arrive at school, and throughout the day. When you're greeting students on the announcement speaker, meeting parents, or discussing an issue with staff, make sure you give off positive energy and enthusiasm. This will carry you through hard times and set the tone for student education. If you want your students to be excited about learning, you'd better be able to show excitement for your duties.

9. Be early to work in the a.m. . . . and recognize anyone there before you.

I've been a morning person my whole life. Even in college while my buddies were partying, I slipped off to bed because I always woke up early. As principal I get to work early—usually around 6:30 a.m. each day is when I arrive. I have some seasoned veterans who are grinders and also get to school early each day. I also have a couple of newcomers. I respect these people immensely, not only because of their work ethic but their dedication to the school, their students, and their careers. I believe getting to work early shows discipline, dedication, and commitment. Do it. Frame your evenings so you can wake up early and get to school. It says a lot. If this is not something that comes naturally to you, work at it. Move the alarm up five minutes a week until you're getting to work when you need to be there.

10. Don't be timid.

As principal you make many decisions that affect the lives of your school community. Be strong. Be confident. Remember that while it is important to listen, understand, and consider others, being timid could be your downfall. Be sensitive but firm. Keep an open mind, but know when it is time to put your foot down. Don't be timid.

Most of you were or will be assistant principals before taking the helm, and there is a big difference between making suggestions and making decisions. You may be wondering, How do I avoid being timid? (Especially if you easily get butterflies in your stomach.) The answer to this is the same as to many of the Wisdom Points in this book. Work at it. Practice your speeches and role-play your meetings. Look at yourself in the mirror, take deep breaths, and believe it is impossible to fail. Yes, act as if there is no risk of you losing. When you can do that, you will believe in yourself; and when you believe in yourself, you will have confidence. If you feel timid, act brave anyway. Once you start behaving differently, your actions will ease your nerves and you'll be better each time.

11. Become tech savvy.

Technology is ever-changing and advancing, and so must you. You have to keep pace with the times. I don't care if you are 29 or 59—get with it. Whatever new technology may look like at the time you are reading this book, get going. If you are motivated to achieve a secure position at a school in a great district, make no mistake, those jobs are competitive. You can't claim to be keeping up with the latest teaching techniques and education trends if you are stuck in a technology rut.

It's easy to get comfortable with what we already know, but don't get stuck. Keep learning. Pay attention, try to have an open mind, and be willing to change. If you don't know someone who can teach you, schedule appointments for tech training. Professional associations and local agencies can teach you the new ways of doing things. If you get stale, people around you will sense it and easily fall into the same habits.

As I sit and write this in the St. Louis airport today, I think about how our new assistant principal, Tom Rickard, pushed me to get more into Google. I was very comfortable with Word, and I admit kind of afraid of Google; but he pushed me to go Google; and we even started a Twitter account for the school. We now have a Google classroom for the staff, we go to special trainings, all our staff meetings are on Google slides, and many of the shared docs are Google docs.

I am aware that Google has its limitations like anything else, but for a public NYS high school, we're moving forward with technology. I am using a Microsoft tablet to write this book, and more often than not have my iPad by my side. Gotta be

FIGURE 1.1 Article by Jessica Cohen for *The Gazette*. Used with permission.

familiar with the tech mix. When you remain a student your-self to keep pace with the technical world, you'll be a better leader for it.

12. Get a mentor.

Who's your girl? Who's your guy? Someone you trust, someone who will guide and advise you as you manage all the stuff com-ing your way. This person can be in your school, your district, or elsewhere, but make sure of one thing: they are/were good at their job. Let me rephrase that: excellent. You want role models who have reached the top of their game so they can give you wise, practical feedback and advice. This is extremely important, because you want to be excellent. That is why you are reading this book, right? You want to be the best, so get a good mentor.

Many times it happens organically, but don't be afraid to ask someone to be your mentor. It is a high compliment to trust their judgment and want to follow their example. Ask questions. Present possible situations and flat-out ask, What would you do when . . . a teacher has an affair with a student, there is a flood at school, a student is caught cheating on a state exam, a student dies at school, nine students are arrested at the school in one day for drugs, and so on.

13. Look the part. Dress to the nines.

I remember walking the hall with Tony DiMarco, the principal who hired me, during my interview. We bumped into Kevin Birmingham in the hall. (Mr. Birmingham is one of our best teachers ever.) Tall, witty, and quirky, he jokingly said to Mr. DiMarco, "I'd hire him. I don't know if he's good or not, but he looks great!"

This stuck with me, and I see it now both as principal and as a college basketball official. If you dress the part, people instantly respect you, because you look like you know what you are doing. I love my comfy jeans and New Balance sneakers as much as anyone, but at work, I dress the part. Pressed shirt, athletic cut slacks, nice shoes (I'm a Clarks guy), and always a well-knotted tie. It is important that you always look neat and presentable. I'm not a big suit guy, but when I do wear them, I make sure they fit right and are in good condition. I visit my friend Maureen at the tailor shop in Milford, PA, and she takes care of me. Go ahead: Ask your kids and be prepared. They will always be honest. Find out if it is time to upgrade the wardrobe, and if they say yes, do it.

This reminds me again of Tom Bongiovi. Tom was principal when I was assistant principal, and now he is superintendent. "Mr. B," as we fondly call him, is a pretty formal gentleman. He wears penny loafers, fancy suits, shirt and tie, and so on. A younger superintendent, yes, but old-fashioned in nature, Mr. B tells his administrators not to loosen their tie until they get on the interstate toward home. His philosophy is to look and act the part. If people see you disheveled or out of sorts, that will change their perception of you in a negative way. Look sharp and put together. You are always the principal here, and you can loosen up after you are well away from school.

14. Conduct frequent headline tests.

Everything you do will be scrutinized. This is all the time, but especially during emergency or high-stress situations. Ask yourself, What would the headline look like if _____? Fill in the blank with: I was caught changing grades. I hired an unqualified person. I was caught in a DUI. I did not suspend the school board president's child. You get the idea.

Run the "headline test" for any and all situations that may occur. It will help you to be prepared, make good decisions, and keep out of trouble. I also use the headline exercise when dealing with students and teachers, because each decision and interaction will be analyzed, evaluated, and judged. What do you do if a teacher has an affair with a student? What do you do if a staff member is a registered sex offender? What if your honors classes have a cheating scandal? You have to react promptly, appropriately, and communicate effectively in all situations. You are the principal. It is up to you to take charge.

I recently had a situation with an athletic team at my school. Some of the athletes were chanting "Mein Kampf" in the locker room showers. When I first became aware of this I was honestly confused, like what the heck? Why would they do such a thing? Then my mind shifted gears, quickly, to, Okay, how do we handle this?

With all that is going on in the world right now—the election of a new president, racist shootings, hate crimes an almost weekly occurrence, and so on, we had to react appropriately. This was a sensitive issue and had to be dealt with swiftly and sternly. Here's what I did:

1. Met with my team and the coaches to get the facts straight.
2. Met with the team midday (the next day) to intensely reprimand them and warn them about what they had done. All coaches and both assistant principals were present.
3. I met with multiple faculty members who are Jewish, to make sure they knew that we were taking this seriously, and it would not be swept under any rug.
4. Sent a letter to all the parents of players on the team, detailing exactly what had happened. Can you imagine if this were a headline on the cover of the newspaper? I'd be appalled.

I remind my team and myself constantly that even if we do nothing wrong, if we do not handle these situations immediately and appropriately, we can easily be in trouble. It is our job to get it right and stay out of the headlines.

15. Go to professional conferences.

When I started as principal, attending conferences didn't seem to be a priority. I was so focused on making things right in my building, I didn't want to miss a day, a class, or a lunch period to attend a program outside the school. I wanted to be there, believed that everything I needed to know was within those walls; but now with a little more wisdom, patience, (and gray hair), I like to go. I am selective about which events I attend, and I have come to recognize that it's important to continue improving at this job. At a good conference you can meet people for effective networking, learn a lot, or sometimes maybe learn just one thing, a big thing that changes how you see and approach certain things from now on.

One important thing I took away from a professional learning conference is the ability to manipulate and change the schedule without having a union issue. We've since created multiple versions of our daily schedule that allow us to have assemblies and events at school without missing class time. Plan the calendar with your secretary and get to a good conference at least once a year.

16. Never miss a chance to shine.

As principal, you are in the spotlight at all times—graduation, bus dismissal, faculty meetings, during classroom observations. . . . Display your leadership talent without showing off or bragging. Let stakeholders remember why they hired you and believe in you. Speak up at meetings; give input. In the cafeteria, talk to the kids. On the loudspeaker, be charming and engaging. In classrooms, give demo lessons or poignant feedback to the staff. You are there to be a great leader for children and educators alike. There are countless opportunities each day to do this, so don't be timid. My former referee boss, John Clougherty, supervisor of the acc, Atlantic 10 and Colonial Conferences, always told us (his refs) this motto: "Never miss a chance to let them see you shine. Make it happen."

17. Become a great public speaker.

This is a must. Public speaking is something you will do each and every day in a variety of settings. If you aren't comfortable or it doesn't come naturally to you, start working on it right away. You will be speaking in front of classes, auditoriums, graduations, funerals, and more. You'll have plenty of opportunities to practice and find your style. Some people do better reading a prepared statement, while others have a gift for improv, and they can speak without a script. I like to have a brief list, a reminder of my talking points, in front of me; essentially a hybrid of a prepared speech for an organized message with off-the-cuff, informal delivery style. Be loud, strong, and keep their attention. As you practice, you'll get better. Ask a brutally honest, critical friend to judge your speeches and give you pointers. Ask teachers you trust to take good notes on your speaking and give you feedback. If you work at getting better, you will.

18. Remember that facts tell, stories sell.

Gotta have good stories and pick the best times to share them. My good friend, Dr. Gilbert, says, "Learn to tell the right story at the right time to the right people."

People will remember your story and not necessarily your speech, so find the stories that make your point and learn to tell them in an entertaining fashion. A favorite that I always share with new staff is how I got hired. I was a first-year graduate student at Wagner College in Staten Island, observing classes at a local high school. Keeping my head down and listening to the morning program, I suddenly heard my name paged over the loudspeaker. The main office secretary was calling me to the principal's office. Whaaaat? Did I do something wrong?

The principal brought me into his spacious office and asked me to sit in front of him. To me, his desk was as big as an aircraft carrier. He informed me that the teacher I was observing had just quit that morning and asked me if I wanted the job. Really? Me? I don't know how to teach, I'm a graduate student just getting started.

I answered, confused, stating, "Well, how would that work? I'm not even certified yet." Then the principal said, "No problem, you'll be certified tomorrow and you can start the next day." OMG!

"Can I make a phone call?" I asked. He said sure, but he needed to know my answer right away, so he could make arrangements for the expedited certification. I called my parents and asked what they thought, and they right away encouraged me to go for it. I explained to them that I would not student teach and ease into it but would start in a full-on teaching position right away. They reminded me that this was how I had learned to swim years before, when the instructor threw me in the pool and told me to start paddling. I hung up the phone, said yes, and off I went, and then proceeded to get my ass kicked for the next eight months. Eventually I figured it out and survived. My audience always gets a kick out of that story, so I enjoy telling it. Collect your stories and tell them. Facts tell, stories sell.

19. Don't write angry e-mails. . . . Never hit send.

This is not only a rule for your professional life, but for life in general. You should never, ever write a mean or angry e-mail. It is simply never a good thing to do. No matter how mad you get, when you want to punch those keys and hit Send, don't do it. We call them nasty grams. Some people I have worked with like to do this on Fridays at 3:00 p.m. Really?

Now don't get me wrong. Writing a nasty gram can be helpful on several levels: It helps you vent and clear your head, organize your thoughts, and release frustration you may have. Just don't hit Send. Never hit Send. If you really want the intended recipient to see it, have someone in the Kitchen Cabinet (see Tip 35) read it and maybe tone it down.

Consider what you are trying to accomplish. Think carefully about your goal for the situation and if what you've written will get you closer to that goal. Chances are you are better off keeping it to yourself. Don't hit Send!

20. Be witty, not sarcastic. Gotta be able to dance.

Learning to say the right thing to the right person at the right time is a skill that comes easier to some than others. Some people have natural instincts for effective communication. Others struggle to find the right words to say in the many situations they face each and every day. I am a firm believer that if you do not know what to say, don't say anything. You cannot get criticized for silence, and you will never regret the moments you kept your mouth shut.

That said, in the constant onslaught of words, questions, dilemmas, decisions, and people coming at you, it helps if you can learn to be witty. Work on lines that you can give back to people when they come at you, so you are always prepared and calm without being or sounding like a pompous ass. Look and sound sharp, but do not mistake careless and sarcastic for witty and charming. It can often be considered rude and disrespectful.

As Tony DiMarco taught me, you have to be able to dance with your words and navigate difficult conversations. Don't be phony, always be genuine and sincere, but be able to dance. Use humor, stories, well-timed pauses, looks, smiles, and great words in your conversations to be an effective communicator.

21. Pass the credit and take the blame.

Learn this habit: When good things happen, pass the credit; when bad things happen, take the blame. This is something good leaders do naturally.

I watched all the interviews with Hall of Fame Coach, Bill Belichick, after the Patriots won their fifth Super Bowl earlier this year. The first thing he said after accepting the Super Bowl trophy was he had to thank his players and assistant coaches for doing a great job. Classy and professional.

A lot of good things will happen on your watch. There are milestones, school achievements, successful concerts and plays, and sports victories, to name a few. You must portray the same leadership qualities in good times and bad. Pass the credit and accept the blame. This speaks again to a "Captain of the Ship" mentality. Your actions determine if and how people respect you; and when you share credit while owning blame, you are respected as a true leader without having to draw attention to yourself.

22. Show strength and confidence.

When the sh*t hits the fan, you have to step up. One day earlier this year a parent jumped out of his truck and approached a young man on campus, and threatened the student, stating, "You are the one who told my daughter to s*ck your _____! You're going to get it you little _____!" The man was crazed and stormed into the front office, demanding to see me. My front office clerk had that look in her eye like, "Oh no, get out of here, Andrew."

I met the man in the foyer and he immediately started yelling. I slowly and firmly told him that I would meet with him if he calmed down. I suggested he take five minutes to breathe and then I would see him. I spoke carefully and deliberately. The man kept saying he was calm, but he wasn't, and eventually I told him he had to leave. He was angry but he did leave, because I was not going to have a screaming match in my office. It was also important to show those who work in the front office that no matter what comes up, I can handle it with poise and strength. We called over to the district office to let them know that they probably had an angry parent coming, which they did, but I took care of the situation right away.

23. The best teachers are the ones who never forget what it's like to be a student . . . and the best principals never forget what's it's like to be a teacher.

In the lines below write down ten things you have loved about teaching and ten things you have disliked about it. Now, look at your teachers. They probably have many of the same likes and dislikes, so keep those close to your heart.

_____

_____

_____

_____

_____

_____

_____

_____

_____

_____

Yes, you are the boss, but this is not a reason to be rude, intimidating, or noncommunicative and difficult to reach. Some of the greatest irritants to teachers are a principal not acknowledging their voice or opinion, unexpected curveballs thrown their way, things promised and not done, interrupting class time, and so on. Know the irritants and try to avoid them at all costs.

If you need to do some things that get under your teachers' skin, communicate with your teacher leaders about what and why. Maybe they can offer a different solution. Use phrases like: I understand; I support you; I remember that when I was a classroom teacher; I can relate, and so on.

Memos that come late on a Friday; long, negative faculty meetings; addressing the whole faculty for the mistakes of one or two people; messing with their classroom space—all these things annoy and frustrate teachers. Make sure they know that you remember what it's like to be in their shoes, facing the issues and challenges that they deal with each day.

24. Meet them where they are.

You have all types: veteran teachers of 30 years with a great attitude; fifth-year teachers who turned sour right after they got tenure; those who get nervous when you enter the room; and those who prance when you walk in the door like they have something to prove. There are some who are always late and unprepared, and others who follow every rule of the school—including driving the 15 mph speed limit when you are behind them and late for a meeting.

The point here is, your staff are at a variety of places in their lives and teaching careers, so meet them where they are. The veteran teacher who's been in the classroom for 25 years may have a hard time adjusting to a new smartboard, while a third-year teacher may know the latest technology but hasn't developed the instincts that only get sharper with time and experience.

Know this and understand it. You do not have to treat everyone the same; but you do have to treat everyone fairly. You can have different kinds of conversations with your staff, depending on where they are at in their lives and careers. Meet them where they are.

25. When you speak, be like a comet: BRIEF + BRILLIANT = MEMORABLE.

This is another tip from my good friend and Hall of Fame teacher, Kevin Birmingham. He gave me this tip when I first started, and I have it tucked in my pocket every time I speak in public:

"Leave 'em yearning for more and never, 'I can't wait for this blowhard to shut his face!'"

26. Don't just be inside your school . . . be INTO your school.

There is a big difference between roaming the halls past children you barely know, and owning the building, aware of everything going on with every kid in every corner. Many school administrators have great attendance and are in school every day, but that doesn't mean they show up on the level required for trusted and respected leadership. Are you in school or into school? What does this mean?

Dr. Gilbert describes it as a simple secret: "It doesn't matter your title, your training, your schooling, etc. It matters what you put into it." This is one of the biggest messages in his work. Be into it. Share confident energy and your enthusiastic, positive mind-set is contagious. People will notice and want to be around you, work with you, work for you.

27. The secret of your success lies in the small things you do every day.

One of the great things about our profession is that we get to repeat the same actions in a similar manner each day. You establish a routine and then adjust it as needed.

Consider this list of things that you can do each day to be successful:

- ◆ Eat a donut.
- ◆ Make at least one good phone call home.
- ◆ Be in at least five classrooms per day.
- ◆ Never be too busy to exercise.
- ◆ Jump right into the day without a rigid schedule.
- ◆ Argue back and forth with a teacher in the hallway.

- Take five minutes to prep for your afternoon meeting with the superintendent.
- Drink plenty of water and eat small meals throughout the day.
- Close your door for two hours to catch up on backed up work you have not addressed.
- Hold a brief planning meeting with your administrative team early in the day.
- Send out a reminder e-mail about the afternoon faculty meeting.
- Have that second soda at dismissal for a little pick-me-up.

From the list above, which can you do each day that will help you? What will help you work better, as a more productive leader? Take a few minutes and write in the lines below the specific actions that will make your daily routine both reliable and flexible. Jot down the small things that make up the secret to your success.

Smile, be kind, keep positive, greet students by their names, follow up with staff and parents on any outstanding questions or issues, eat healthy, drink water, exercise, and so on. Feel free to take some or all of my suggestions and make them your own, then add more of your own items as you discover what works for you. Soon enough you will filter and confirm your own custom list that will serve as a healthy foundation for each new day.

_____

_____

_____

_____

_____

_____

_____

_____

28. Take the heat for the superintendent and your AP(s) take the heat for you.

One of your many tasks is to take heat off the superintendent. Your AP(s) should help take heat off you. It trickles down from there. You do not want calls going to the Sup for problems or situations that you could/should have handled. Ensure that unnecessary calls don't go to the Sup. Make it a priority that he or she is not going to get more work or more headaches because of your shortcomings. No more crap on his or her desk because you couldn't handle a problem, or worse, you caused a problem. Handle your business and keep it out of the superintendent's office.

Furthermore, have the expectation that your assistant principal(s) will handle the business that they should, to keep you freed up to be the principal. If you are consistently bogged down with simple discipline issues or items that they should handle on their own, you will have a hard time. Empower your AP(s) to take care of things so they will rise to your level of expectation and keep work off your desk by doing whatever they can on your behalf.

One funny story (it wasn't funny then): When I was a young AP, we were fighting smoking in our building, and it was an uphill battle. I was crazed, in and out of bathrooms, checking smoke detector beepers, and doing all I could to make sure the rules were enforced and respected. I saw a student with whom I'd had multiple run-ins, usually after catching him getting ready to light up on the sidewalk. I approached quickly and yelled, "Hey" and called his name. The student was startled and quickly hid the cigarette. I told him to hand it over, but he played dumb and denied having one. I demanded the cigarette and grabbed it out of his hand, at which point the cigarette ripped in half as he clenched his fist to conceal it. In the frustration of the moment, I grabbed his hand in addition to the cigarette. Well, you can guess how this is going from here. He yelled, "Get your f*cking hands off me!" and "Don't touch me!" and all sorts of dramatic pleas for attention. I told him he was being suspended and he stormed off to call his parents.

It was spirit week and I was wearing a Peyton Manning jersey at the time. Sure enough, the boy and his parents went to the superintendent's office to claim that I had assaulted the student and they wanted a piece of me. This didn't look good. I scrounged around, asking anyone for a shirt and tie. Most people were in jerseys like I was. My principal at the time was my good friend, Tony DiMarco. He had an old, checkered, red and black short sleeve shirt and a navy blue tie . . . Really? That was my only option. I put it on and looked like an old, wrinkled tablecloth.

Needless to say, I didn't feel great going into that meeting.

In hindsight, many years and tense situations later, I've learned that my zealous desire to enforce the rules in those early days did not help me find the best approach to that situation. I got creamed at the meeting because I was too aggressive in trying to get the cigarette. Additionally, I looked like a picnic table!

What would I do differently now? What do I know now that I didn't know back then?

Take five minutes and write down all the things that you think I could have done differently in this situation. I have written my thoughts on the next page. Let's see how closely we match. No peeking!!

_____

_____

_____

_____

_____

_____

_____

_____

_____

_____

_____

_____

_____

_____

1. Stay calm.
2. Ask for the cigarette.
3. Clearly explain that I saw it in his hand and a lighter in the other.
4. Explain that the code of conduct reads that if a student flees or refuses to be searched, we can punish as if they are guilty of possessing what we suspect in the first place. (Know the rules. I did not know this at the time!)
5. Get in touch with the student's parents right there on the spot; get them involved earlier.
6. Do not ever touch the student.
7. Bring a second adult to join me as a witness.
8. Call the superintendent and let them know they might be getting a complaint.
9. Have a spare shirt and tie in the office at all times.

29. Be the first source of information during a time of crisis.

In the age of 24/7 social media and real-time digital Breaking News, it can be tough to be the first source people turn to; but you do not want Facebook or some random blog releasing news about your school before you present it yourself. You want your office to be the first place people turn to for information in a time of crisis. Get out in front of it and face the music: good or bad. There might be lawyers or bosses telling you not to make a statement for one reason or another, so you may have to navigate that; but get out in front of it as quickly as you can and be the reliable, honest source of updates on the situation at hand. Be quick, but not in a hurry. Be accurate, but cautious about giving all the information to the general public. Be prepared and get the news out: e-mail blast, public meeting, letter home, video release, and so on. Don't let others do this for you. When a dangerous or scary situation arises, you have to be a leader the community can turn to and trust for timely, accurate information.

2

Remember the Premium Value of People and Relationships

30. Learn people's names and their kids' names to interact with commitment to caring.

This may seem obvious, but it is not an easy skill, especially if interacting with people does not come naturally to you. Greeting someone by name goes a long way toward connecting with people and earning their respect—two of your big jobs. If you have to work at it, start asking people their names and repeat it when they tell you. Say their name aloud and write it down somewhere. When you call someone that you just met by his or her name the next time you see that person, they will feel an instant connection. Wow, he already knows my name. He cares. That was fast! Practice, work at it, and do not be afraid to ask people when you forget, because you will and that's okay. Tell them you are working on it and you'll get it.

31. Learn something about every family. What makes them tick?

Are they huge, generational Buffalo Bills fans; did they just ride their bikes across the country; did they lose a child early in life; do they want to lose weight? If you don't get to know people, you will be disconnected, and it is nearly impossible to lead a school community as an outsider. Imagine if you didn't know someone was trying to lose weight or worried about their eating habits, and you brought them a box of donuts to be nice. How would that go over? In their minds you'd be an idiot, an insensitive jerk. In your mind, you went out of your way to treat someone you work with. This is a well-intended misunderstanding.

Study people, know them. The business of education and school leadership is all about relationships. If you treat people with simple respect and kindness, they will do most anything for you. When you take it a step further and ask people about themselves, their families, and their lives, it shows that you care and have an investment in them as members of the community you lead.

A story that is near and dear to me is from when I lost my father. It was November 2008, and we had just completed our fourth marathon together with my brother. Dad died that night when he returned home, and I spent the next whole week with family and friends, celebrating his life and mourning his passing. I was exhausted when I returned home and took off that following Monday. When I finally returned to school on Tuesday, the first thing I did was check my voice mail messages.

The first message was from my superintendent, John Xanthis, asking how my dad and I had done at the marathon. John knew my dad and I were really close, and what walking with him in that marathon meant to me. He obviously did not know when he left the message that Dad had passed away.

That message really hit me. John probably had 25 things to do that morning, but he called me first thing to let me know he was thinking of my family. I saved it for the rest of the year and listened to it multiple times. It helped me through a tough time because it was clear that he cared.

32. Hire GREAT people.

One of the most important jobs you have is to hire fantastic people. Your staff is your single most important resource, because they have the greatest impact on your students. It is the people, people, and the people that make your school what it is.

Invest your time and energy to run a tight interview process. Sit with people who will help you interview and brainstorm: What is it that you are looking for? What characteristics do you need and want in the person for this position?

I am not a big fan of huge interview committees. I suggest choosing one, two, or three people to join you, and don't be afraid to mix up the committee. Different people offer a variety of perspectives. Put time in to review the applications, keep interviews moving, and don't hesitate to have a second round if you aren't sure. I call it the "walk and talk"—inviting two or three people back for a second round, to stroll around the building and talk. Ask about their families, their likes, dislikes, and so on. See how they interact with staff and students. Do they look people in the eye when they meet them? Did they repeat their names to try and remember them? Do they tell a good story, or only try to top others' stories?

You can tell a lot from walk and talk interviews. It is one of my favorite things to do with candidates, to see if and how they fit in. I intentionally throw some curveballs to see how they react, like a student asking, "How would you deal with a student who curses at you?" Or, "What's your philosophy on cell phones in school?" I get to see if they act differently when meeting the superintendent or a custodian. Do they treat the head custodian differently than a regular custodian?

You learn a lot about a person when you watch them in a casual, semi-controlled setting. We were once doing a walk and talk with a recent candidate for a position. He did well in the initial interview, and we brought him back to meet some people on a walk and talk. When I introduced him to a teacher in the building, after cordial greetings, she asked him very simply, "Where are you from?" He paused for two or three seconds before he answered. It was a very odd moment, and it made me think, How could he not answer that? Was he hiding something? His hesitation over such a simple question was a red flag, and I picked another candidate. Be prepared, stay calm, proceed with confidence, and hire great people who will strengthen and enhance your school community.

33. Don't promise people jobs.

As principal, you have many people trying to influence you and your decisions for a variety of reasons: personal gain, something for their child, less or more of something from you, and many times, trying to get a family member or friend hired. When you go into interview time, regardless of the position, make it public, loud and clear, from the superintendent to the newest assistant, part-time school monitor, that you are hiring the best person for the job, period. Make this one of your mottos and let everyone know. If someone pressures you, respond that you would be happy to meet anyone, but you and your interview team will be making the selection based on specific criteria, and personal introductions are not on the list. Also, be clear with your interview team that this is not a democracy. Request and welcome their input, but you make the final decision.

One of the biggest keys to your success and your legacy in the school is whom you've hired. You do not want to be tied to a favor for someone. If a candidate is not up to the challenge or just not the best fit, have the courage to tell the person who is pushing you that they need to back off and leave it alone.

34. Call good candidates back to discuss why they didn't get the job.

This is a courteous, kind, helpful thing you can do for people who come close but don't quite make it to getting hired. Your feedback can be a valuable lesson, especially for young people interviewing just after college. It takes a little bit of time out of your day, but it can go a long way in fostering someone else's success. You also never know when your paths may cross again, and that person will always remember that you took the time to call and speak with them.

35. Develop your Kitchen Cabinet for a reliable crew of advisors.

Who do you trust to bounce new ideas off of? Who offers you perspective? The Kitchen Cabinet. I took this title from friend and mentor, John Xanthis. We fondly call him X-man. You will notice X-man is mentioned several times in this book.

Maybe your idea is good one, but your timing is off or you are planning to deliver your message in the wrong place. The Kitchen Cabinet is your own personal Advisory Board, people who will listen to your ideas and give honest feedback without any hidden agenda. Trust those closest to you and hear them out; even if you disagree and don't always take their suggestions, it is helpful to entertain dissenting conversations with people you trust and respect. It keeps your mind open and your motives honest. It also gets your wheels turning and keeps you think-ing in different directions for best ways to serve your school. Deciding who belongs in your Kitchen Cabinet is a good thing to start early.

36. Give people chances, but not too many.

You are in the people business of building and maintaining relationships—forging bonds with teenagers, no less, who are often so at odds with themselves it is hard to get them to have faith in any authority figure. Whether a situation is regarding adults or students or both, give people chances, most especially the students. Many times, people expect you to come down hard with punishments and such, but is that what's most effective? Is that what's best for the student or staff member?

Two quick stories:

1. A boy cursed at a teacher who was walking down the hall. The teacher tried to stop the boy, and again, the boy cursed at him, then began screaming. We found out later that the boy had just spoken to his dad, who told him that his mother had passed away. . . . Should that boy have been punished? Did he deserve a second chance? Certainly I believe he did, and you have to be ready to listen and understand all factors before making important decisions.

2. "Mrs. Nyland, this is just a little appreciation gift from me and my family. Since I came to PJHS I can say you have helped me so much and as you say 'babied' me a lot. Thank you for all your help. God bless. Love, mdj"

The writing above is a note from a student to Mrs. Nyland, our award-winning assistant principal. Mrs. Nyland goes above and beyond for our students and staff. She was very patient with this student over the years. The young lady was a potential dropout, and Mrs. Nyland stayed the course with her. She gave her multiple chances and eventually it paid off. My point is, chances are not to be unlimited or taken lightly, but sometimes people need and deserve some extra help. Some students or teachers or parents may need more chances than you really want to give, but with Mrs. Nyland's patience and help, this girl graduated and is now on to a successful career. We are in a unique position to effect change in young people's lives, and that is something we can never forget, underestimate, or ignore.

37. Write it up and then rip it up.

One technique I developed is the "rip up." This is something I do when I'm not happy with a veteran teacher's observation. Some of the more experienced teachers may not put their best foot forward during an announced observation. Here are your options:

1. Write the observation as is and give it to the teacher.
2. Sugarcoat the observation and do not make it out as bad as it was.
3. Turn a blind eye and write up a generic observation.
4. Write an honest observation and let the teacher know your thoughts and expectations, then rip it up and give them another crack at it.

I believe this practice lets you accomplish the ultimate goal of getting a teacher to respect and do what you ask in the classroom, without having a black mark on their record. By giving them a re-do, you are respecting their years and experience while still making it clear that you expect them to comply with requests. Now, this is only a once or maybe twice act, so as always it depends on the character of the person you're dealing with and their desire to make it work; but I have seen that this is a great way to build better relationships with your teachers. When they don't hit the mark you set, give them honest feedback along with a second chance. When you combine clear communication of expectations with space and freedom to make their choice again in the future, it is a fair, courteous, and efficient approach.

Note: You should actually rip the papers up. It adds impact to your meeting with the teacher when you literally show that you are giving them another chance.

38. Focus on strong relationships with key people.

There are several people you will do well to focus on as you build professional relationships across your school community. Be respectful to everyone you work with, but develop extra special bonds with your head custodian, head nurse, lead secretary, and PTSA president. These people have a significant influence on whether or not you can succeed in your position. They make a lot happen in and around the building. Treat them well, acknowledge their work, and make them feel appreciated so they want to do a good job for the school, the staff, the kids, and in the end, you.

38A. Meet with key school people on a regular basis— Board of Education president, head of B&G (buildings and grounds), head custodian, and so on.

People are flying fast through each day. Life is hectic; we all have a list of things on our minds. Stop, and pause to talk with people. Invite them in for coffee or lunch; invest some time with the key stakeholders in your building and the district. So many people only communicate with e-mail or texting. Don't lose the magic of direct conversation: a look in the eye, a handshake, a tear, a laugh, sincerity. They're all there in any conversation, so meet with your people. Bring them into your fold. You'll create a better environment for everyone who works there, and you'll be happy you did.

I remember years ago when I was up for tenure as assistant principal. There was a split board at the time with some issues going on in the district, and it was possible that I was not going to get tenure due to a number of factors, most of which had nothing to do with me or my job performance. One board member contacted my principal at the time, and asked to meet with me. Everyone was shocked. No way! Fuggetaboutit!

I thought about it, and realized, What do I have to lose? I had already accepted that he was going to vote No without even meeting me, so if a meeting might change his mind, it couldn't hurt. We set it up and I met with the gentleman, and it went great. He shared a number of things that he had heard about me, and asked me to speak on them. This was fair, and I was thrilled.

One thing he said was that he had heard I had an anger management problem. Whaaat? I knew that this came from a short list of disgruntled parents and students who had definitely heard me raise my voice. One in particular I flat-out yelled at. (That student would later wind up going to prison for drugs.)

I asked the board member, "Do you think the AP should be able to raise his voice in response to certain situations?" (This was a moment for a little extra mustard!) "Do you think the students should have a tiny bit of fear/healthy respect for the AP? Do you want this place cleaned up?"

There is a certain freedom in having nothing to lose. I was completely honest and was myself, and our conversation went great. We both left that meeting with more respect for one another than when we went in, and I did eventually get tenure (by a slim margin!). Sitting down and meeting with that BOE member went a long way in helping me. You will never be sorry to have allies, or at least to know the people you are working with, beyond a computer screen.

38B. This cannot be overstated. Honor and trust your AP or AP(s).

You will only be as good as your AP(s). I believe many principals have two or more APs, but of course this isn't always the case. If you have none, God bless you!

Your APs are your eyes and ears. They are the closest extension of you, and they can make you or break you. If they are strong, give them the latitude to run with new projects, develop ideas, and do their thing. Empower them. Build them up and let them shine. Give them credit at every turn. Listen to them, support them, and promote them. You are training them each day to be a principal, so be a role model for them. They're watching you, so show them how to do it. Have them sit in on difficult meetings with you and share memos so they can see how you write them. Setting an example will help them and urges you to always be at your best. This builds a trusting partnership between you as together you lead the way for the school.

I say often that it is lonely at the top. When you're the boss there is a natural tendency for people to shy away, or simply have a rule not to like you because you are the boss. Well, you need and want your APs with you, by your side and ready to work, so be sure to invest in them as professionals, and in those relationships.

The flip side of this is if your APs are weak or ineffective.

If this happens, and it certainly does, I'm sorry to say it, but you're in trouble. If you hired them, shame on you. If you inherited them, get busy. You can do one of two things: work on helping them to improve, or work on getting rid of them. Either choice here benefits both you and the school.

What you cannot do is leave them be. A bad AP will sink the ship with you in it. Getting rid of an employee is a painstaking ritual, but it is the way of schools and teacher unions, so get used to it.

People will respect you for demanding excellence in your co-leaders. If you choose to support and assist that person or people, start with a clear outline. Meet with them with a union representative and clearly communicate your concerns. Some places call this a PIP (Principal Improvement Plan). Let them know that you want to make them better and that you will give them a genuine opportunity to do so; but if they do not change the things you talk about in X amount of time, you will start the disciplinary process and support will end.

Be clear that you are not there yet, but will go there if they are not willing to change, or not capable of changing.

38C. Get to know key people in the community.

The superintendent, the mayor, the police chief, the hospital administrator, the fire department, the top pizzeria (very important!), the recreation director, the council people, the pastor, the district attorney, the scoutmaster, the funeral home director, the newspaper reporter, and so on. Do you know who these people are? Do you have their cell numbers? Their e-mail addresses? If so, great. If you do not, get on it; meet them, become acquainted, buy a round of coffee, spend a half hour. It is important in emergency situations that you can have a direct line open to these other community leaders. Don't wait for something to happen when you need someone. Take time to meet them in person because it is the right thing to do, to respect their role in the community, as you hope they will respect yours. Chances are as local professionals they have had or have children of their own attending your school. Once you make direct contact and have a genuine conversation, show that you care and want to have a positive alliance with them, you can gain access to them and they get access to you.

I'm not suggesting you connect with local officials like in the Mafia movies, but connect in a way that you can reach them quickly and effectively when needed. Example: Driving to work I hit a huge pothole on the turn into the school. There was construction the day before, and the workers missed a spot in patching up. I pulled over right away and texted the mayor, who was on it in a flash. It was fixed before dismissal the same afternoon.

Another time we had to face the death of a former student. The family was not well off financially, and needed some assistance. I was able to connect them with community members to assist with funeral services including our photo person for the school, who arranged to have a beautiful photo of the student at the services. It was a nice touch. I was able to introduce these people quickly because I had their numbers and had developed relationships with them over time. It always comes back to valuing people and being valuable to them: a reliable source of information, support, and assistance. That is the job.

38D. Treat your secretary like gold.

I learned as a young man to treat girls as I wanted my sisters to be treated, and as I wanted my mom to be treated.

Then I learned to treat my girlfriend like I would want my future wife to be treated, and I did. I treated my girlfriend like she would be my future wife, and she became my wife! That's what happened.

In my work life, I learned pretty quickly that it is essential to treat your secretary like gold. He or she has a big role in your job and how well you will do. That person is your eyes and ears, thermometer, filter, and strategic guide. They help keep you on schedule, proofread your documents, and constantly remind you of the many things that you have to take care of each day.

My secretary, Mrs. Reenie Nicolette, is truly a savior for me. She does it all, assisting with all aspects of my job. On top of helping to manage a hectic office, Reenie has a great heart and genuinely cares how I do. We have cultivated a great working relationship, and I am very blessed to have her help. My point: Don't neglect the one who takes care of you. Treat her or him like gold, try not to overload, buy lunch from time to time, bring flowers and trinkets for the office, and so on. Reenie has helped me tremendously, and that needs to be a two-way street.

39. Go to community events.

You are a busy person, attending staff meetings, class gatherings, school activities, dances, board meetings, graduations; and when your calendar is already bursting, you always need to make time for one more PTA function, basketball game, fundraiser, bake sale. . . . More? How can I possibly have more time? Make it happen. Bring your own kids; work with your family on your schedule after school and on weekends.

One of the most rewarding things I've attended was a young man's Eagle Scout ceremony in my school's community. I was there to honor this student's accomplishments and represent the school in a positive light. I took two of my own children and met the boy's family and friends. It was time well spent. People got to see me outside of school, with my own family, in a different light. People remember these interactions. You can't go to everything, but you can make special efforts to attend these types of events. It's worth it.

40. Do the walk and talk with school guests and visitors.

When you welcome guests to your school, do the walk and talk. Stroll the halls, showing off your great staff, students, and building. You may have an important meeting with this person, so bring them around first and show off your school and your work. Show them how you interact with your people, know all the kids' names, and how you pick bits of paper up from the floor as a natural part of your day. There are conversations that require no words; just a brief walk shows the kind of leader you are to your staff and students. Remember, never miss a chance to shine.

3

School Stuff

Connect With the Kids and Create a Super Dope Culture

41. Adopt a loose and tight mentality to carefully choose your battles.

There are countless rules and regulations in running a school. As principal, you have to decide what you are going to focus on, and prioritize what must be enforced strictly vs. something less serious to obey. Ask yourself, What are some core values that I want my school to stand for?

Is there a dress code issue? A problem with repeat lateness? Staff not parking in the assigned parking spots? Be clear about which rules you will be tight on, and what you are loose on.

A couple of examples at PJHS are: Sitting up front at faculty meetings. I never like people sitting in the back. It isn't fun or productive to speak to a disengaged audience. I always ask them to sit up front; I am pretty tight on that.

An example of being loose is hats. The rule is that students can wear hats in school, but not in the classroom. Our staff has developed the philosophy that as long as students are doing their schoolwork and giving their attention and focus in class, it doesn't really matter to most teachers if some students wear ball caps. We communicated to the students that if a teacher directs them to take the hat off, they have to listen and respect the request, but generally it isn't a big deal.

Loose and tight. This mentality offers some flexibility in how you deal with the myriad of issues that inevitably come up.

42. Create yearly theme slogans and monthly theme days that people can rally behind.

This is a spirit call for staff, students, parents, and the whole school. Choose a theme for each year and use it on your e-mail signature, on your faculty meetup page, on programs and event announcements, and so on. Some examples I have used in the past are: We Are Port Jervis, Enjoy the Journey, Motivate and Inspire, and This Is the Year.

In addition to annual themes, once a month or so put a theme day on the calendar that people can dress up for. This started with our spirit week where students would dress up each day to earn points for their classes. We then had bowtie day, ugly holiday sweater day, and it took off from there. We now have flannel day, destination day, go green day for St. Paddy's, and each Friday is Port Pride day where students and staff wear our school colors.

Get creative and have fun with it. You can run contests, have people vote, give two free tickets to the local movie theater to winners, and so on. We also usually gather at the end of each theme day and take a yearbook photo. Enjoy! This is a small thing you can do that does not cost much, nor is there any score kept. It's just fun.

Themes are a simple yet effective way to bring a sense of unity and solidarity to the student body as well as the staff. People typically welcome something to be a part of, something that effortlessly connects them to others. . . . . They help to keep things fresh and creative for staff who come back year after year doing similar work, which can grow redundant. Theme slogans make each new year something different for everyone in the school, and theme days help classmates to bond while building class pride along with fun memories.

43. Update signs and bulletin boards on a regular basis.

Signs and bulletin boards are usually what guests and visitors see when they step into the building and walk through the halls. You are in charge, and these little things are important. Make sure every feature display, calendar, announcement, and so on, is always up to date.

Think about your school right now. What's on your boards? When was the last time they were updated? Is the paper new? Are the boards clean and neat looking? Are student pictures and achievements posted? Is the information provided both relevant and timely? These details are essential to the efficiency and appearance of your school.

Having bright, colorful, new bulletin boards says a lot about what's happening in your school and the culture of the building. If you allow boards to become ratty and cluttered with outdated announcements and information, it says that other things are probably ratty, too. For the naysayers who claim that "The kids are going to destroy them anyway, so why bother?" I say, you stay on it. Identify where the potential problem could be. If someone rips it up, you fix it. If they rip it up again, you fix it again and address it: Watch the camera feeds, get on the loudspeaker, respond! You will win that battle by being firm and clear that you insist on maintaining nice bulletin boards.

Think about entering a hotel or restaurant that does not look sharp. Would you want to stay or eat there? Probably not. It is the same in your school. Make it look nice. Get artistic people to help you. You can't do it all yourself, but some teachers and students love to make things look pretty, especially in the elementary schools. Find out who those people are and get them on board (pun intended). Get students involved, and not just in September. Update them, fix them, change out the content, and so on. You may think this is minor and insignificant, but it matters. Make those bulletin boards and make them great! This is an expression of care within and for the school.

44. Develop a strong freshman, 6th-grade program, and kindergarten orientation.

The biggest factor in achieving success toward graduation in four years is being on track as a freshman. This one took a few years for me to fully catch on to.

Whenever and wherever you become principal, there are a bunch of things in place that the school has been doing for many years before you arrived. Look at these things right away and determine how each program is run, who runs it, and who else is involved.

A new batch of freshmen in the school requires early and clear communication of expectations. This goes for the parents as well as students, and is very important. Freshmen are like little chickadees running around with no direction. It is like a big spaceship has landed in front of your school and dropped these 13- and 14-year-olds off, and their leader asks you to help them graduate in four years! Freshmen need a lot of attention, and it is your job to ensure they get started with plenty of support.

Whatever level you are on—elementary, middle, or high school—make sure that first year (kindergarten, 6th grade, or 9th) is a smooth transition. Make sure information is readily available so parents and students are put at ease and made to feel comfortable. Get dates and times out early, and plan high-quality, welcoming, engaging orientation programs.

45. Learn how to get things paid for in your school using grants, alumni, the business office, and so on.

Funding is a tricky topic. I said many a time working at my school as principal, "This isn't my dad's pharmacy!"

Public (or private) education is nothing at all like it was in my dad's pharmacy on Staten Island back in the day. Dad was the supreme ruler of his bustling Mom and Pop shop. He ran his business the way he ran his family—he was the man, in every sense. What he said was law. He did what he wanted, when and how he wanted to do it.

In the school system, to be able to spend money on anything, you first have to get it approved, approved, approved—by the superintendent, the BOE (if necessary), the assistant superintendent for business, and, of course, the mother of all that you do—your secretary. There are rules, regulations, and red tape in purchasing any item for a school. What has to be BOE approved? Are there minimum or maximum amounts? Do you need to get bids, etc.?

Ask questions and double check before you authorize a purchase. I am not a fan of doing it first and asking for forgiveness second, especially when it comes to spending money. You never want to have an issue where people accuse you of misappropriating public funds. You can run into all kinds of trouble once you start down the money path, so make sure you process every transaction according to protocols, even if it means extra red tape.

46. Develop transparent policies for parents and students: grades, rules, procedures, how kids get into honors programs, and so on.

Clarity is your friend. You may encounter rules, regulations, and ways of doing things that are ancient, outdated, or just plain ineffective. Look at them all and determine which ones might need minor tweaks, significant adjustments, or total revamping. This in itself may be a challenge.

When you develop transparent policies and regulations, it supports knowledge and awareness for parents and students. People like to know what's going on, what to expect. They want to be clear on how their child can achieve beyond the status quo, get admitted to advanced classes, take care of any prerequisites, and so on. Make this information easy to find and understand. Share necessary facts on school websites and teacher syllabi; have info hanging in classrooms, and available at parent events. Without clarity and transparency, confusion breeds a sense of mistrust. People will accuse you of showing favoritism toward others because their kids got into a certain class or got a role in the play. Don't leave yourself unprotected. When everything is out in the open and clear for all to see, you avoid pitfalls and the risk of people being offended or imagining a slight.

Fear: False Evidence Appearing Real. Yet another gem from my good friend, Tom Bongiovi, Superintendent of Schools in Port Jervis. If people are skeptical or do not believe what teachers and administrators are telling them, fear will settle in. People will make up their own opinions as to why their kid did or did not achieve something, vs. the real reason—they earned it or they didn't. Not only will these simple policies and practices reduce the number of angry people at your office door, but if/when upset parties do complain or question your tactics, you have a clear, professional answer that is out in the open for all to see.

One incident that prompted me to make a change at my school was dealing with the honors criteria—how students were chosen for advanced classes. I had several issues with the way it was set up.

1. The rubric was kept from the parents and students. They did not see it before or after the selection process.
2. The rubric was extremely subjective: Subject knowledge was a category only based on the teacher's opinion.

Shouldn't subject knowledge be determined by a student's grade?

3. Limiting: There was no cutoff in terms of achievement. The cutoff was based on a number of students (25). So if your kid was number 26 and high achieving and deserving, they didn't make it because of space? I did not like that.

We put a group of teachers together and hashed it out and came up with a set of clear, measurable criteria that students had to meet to get into honors. Scoring was 88% average in the class and an 85% on the final. Bam. Simple, transparent. We advertised it for half a year and then put it into place and did not have a lot of kickback. People understood it, and whether they liked it or not, they knew what they needed to do to get into honors. I did not have any parents complaining that this was unfair. No one was confused about the process. It was a positive change.

47. Make the grounds in and around the campus beautiful.

When people arrive at your school, the outside says a lot about what is going on inside. Plant flowerpots, clean the front walkway, and make sure the entryway is neat, uncluttered, and swept. If the outside is dirty, do you think people want to go in there? It's the same for kids. If the school grounds look overgrown and uncared for, this sends a message to students (and parents) that you allow it to remain that way.

48. Greet students and staff in the morning.

Get to the building early and spend some time in the hallway. Meet your staff in the a.m., and shortly after, meet and greet the students. This is not heavy lifting, just being in the right place at the right time. These few minutes before school are when you get chances to speak to your staff about how their children are, how's that extension on the house going, how is the back injury feeling, and how are your classes going. . . . Just be there with a smile, a calm, confident presence, and as a leader who shows up and cares. It goes a long way for your staff to know you're there early, ready to be there for them, ask about them, and listen when they answer. They see you making time for them. Then the bell rings and it's time for students. Get to the best spot to greet them as they pour into the hall. High fives, hugs, hellos, and smiles. Good morning, how are you? Did you do your homework? What time is your game tonight? I love your sweater, I love your new glasses. . . . Those tiny moments of connection are valuable time, so get out there and see your people. They want to see you. Be there for them.

49. When having special events or guests, put up a welcome sign, and greet them at the door.

I learned a lot of lessons from my mom and dad, Dorothy and Joe Marotta. I love them yesterday, today, and forever. They are my heroes, and the best way I can ever repay them is to do the same or better for my children. One of the many things they taught me is to always be ready for guests when you are hosting in your home. Greet them at the door, make sure you have food out, make sure you get them something to drink, and make them feel comfortable. I have adopted this same philosophy at my school. Make your school a warm, inviting, friendly place, as if you are welcoming friends to your home. That is how you should treat guests to the school when you have an event. Get everything ready and take pride in being a prepared and gracious host.

It does not take any special skill to simply say, "Welcome to _____" (your school name). It immediately creates a sense of warmth and shows you care. Add a smile and a genuine hand-shake, and you will represent your school as a winner.

50. Get an "extra clean" before events.

That's right: an extra clean. That's what I call it. If you have the play in the auditorium or a game in the gym, or a meeting in the library to discuss the writing curriculum, get your cus-todial team to give you a little extra cleaning so the area you are in is ready and primed for you. I go back to the restaurant analogy I have used throughout this book: Would you want to eat in a restaurant that looks or feels dirty? The clear-cut answer is no.

51. Order personalized cards and notepaper. Write short notes to people daily.

People crave recognition. No matter how long they've been teaching, it feels good to be appreciated. There are countless opportunities to make people feel special each day: a student wins a school award, a teacher celebrates their 25th wedding anniversary, a custodian gives up smoking . . . whatever the milestone or accomplishment, you can take two minutes to jot a short note that will make someone smile.

52. Set up High-Five Fridays, Free Coffee Fridays, Songs on Friday, and so on.

People are tired at the end of the week, ready for the weekend. By Friday, teachers and students both want the routine of the week to be over, so make Fridays cool and fun. Keep it focused on academics, but add some things that make Fridays a little lighter, and different.

HFF: Get different clubs or groups of students to line up in the hallways five to ten minutes before school starts; and once the other students come into the building, that club or group offers enthusiastic and welcoming high fives to the students. It's a great thing and starts the day or afternoon with some upbeat energy. Also, giving out coffee to staff or playing a popular song at the end of the day over the loudspeaker are other easy ways to give good vibes to the school. This idea was started by our Friends of Rachel club.

53. Plan staff luncheons—bring something to share.

As principal you are always seeking new ways to bring people together. After growing up in an Italian household, I can tell you the best place to do this is around a table with food! Host staff luncheons a few times a year. Most people like to go out on staff development days, so choose a couple times that you'll have a catered lunch or do a potluck. Set parameters, make a shared list, and let people sign up with what they are going to bring. There a several variations you can try for this: bring a recipe for your dish, share a recipe, bring anonymous dishes so people can vote for their favorites, have secret taste tests of the same dishes, soup days, and so on. There are plenty of simple, inexpensive things you can set up to bring your staff together around the table. Food is a daily part of everyone's life, something we all have in common. Be creative and have some fun. Take your foot off the boss pedal in these settings. Relax, be yourself, and enjoy a meal with your staff.

One idea from my art department's chairperson was the empty bowl project. She had the students make ceramic bowls and then asked staff to bring in different kinds of soup. For $10, staff could come, pick out a bowl to keep and sample different soups from the other staff. It was a win for everyone. Staff came together to share food and conversation, the art department ran a successful fundraiser for a local food bank, and the students got to showcase their work. Take this idea and use it as your own. It was a great event for our school.

54. Get into the classrooms constantly and consistently.

This is a top priority. You can (and will) get so busy that sometimes it is easier to just sit in your office and "get your work done." Except that being in the classroom *is* your work. To be an educational leader, not just a building manager, get in there. Every day. Mix up where you go and when you go. Visit brand-new teachers as well as seasoned veterans. When you do this all the time, on a regular basis, the adults become comfortable with it, as well as the students. There should never be a gasp or an awkward silence when the principal walks into a room. It should be a frequent pattern that everyone is used to and okay with. Make it a priority and do it today.

55. Give timely, pointed feedback.

When you give feedback to teachers, be specific and constructive. Not just good job or great to see you today, but marked feedback in a timely fashion. A quick e-mail, a short note in their mailbox, or a walk down the hall goes a long way toward showing that you care and you are paying attention. My team likes to say, "two wows and a now"; meaning one or two positive points with one or two things they can improve on or try differently. This is what teachers want and expect from you. Be present. Help each of them to be their best. Yes, some might joke about leaving them alone and say they are masters of their domain, or claim you are trying to micromanage, but in my many years of experience I have learned that most teachers do want respectful, constructive feedback, so make it a point to make the time.

56. Send reminders . . . people forget.

We live in a very busy world. Cell phone, Internet, apps, e-mails, students, students, and more students. Deadlines, due dates, and so on. Some of your staff are connected. They have digital reminders and all kinds of alerts that will buzz and beep when it is time for something. Others will not check their e-mail for two days. My point: Always send reminders.

People forget. Their minds are on 50 things at once—their job, their spouse, the kids, aging parents, something that needs to be fixed in the house, you name it. The important program that you just spent a month working on, the one that begins at 1:00 p.m.? There are some staff who have forgotten it is even happening, so be aware of this and send reminders—weekly, daily, even hourly. Have a professional development starting at 2:15 p.m. after school? I like to send a first reminder a day or two before, then another the morning of, and again about ten minutes before. Is this overkill? You think it's too much? Maybe, but what is the end result you are looking for? To make people aware of the agenda, time frames, location, and so on, and get them to the meeting.

57. Write to the news and keep in touch with local media for positive press.

Never miss a chance to get your school positive press. Be proactive; contact the paper. Good news is contagious. Unfortunately, many newspapers like to run sensational reports of murders, accidents, and drug deals in the area vs. covering happy stories about local kids and families. Develop relationships with the local paper and radio station; contact their employees a few times each year, so when you need to pick up the phone or shoot an e-mail sharing positive news, they know who you are and will be receptive.

A scholarship to Brown University, reading scores on state tests, Eagle Scout announcements, and so on. Get it out there and share the good stuff. If you send ten newsworthy items, maybe they will run three or four of them, and that is good. You can't expect success 100% of the time on everything you try, but the more you do, the more successes you will see. Keep sending announcements of achievements and milestones, special occasions. Celebrate your school community and share the joy.

58. Clip articles about your students and display them in the school.

We have a board in the school called PJHS in the News. Display your school's news for everyone to see. Furthermore, send a copy home to the student's family with a short, personal, hand-written note congratulating them. This means a lot to kids regardless of their age, and the parents will appreciate your efforts. This falls under "do more than is expected." It takes extra effort, but the end results are worth it.

59. Invite alumni back to the school. Have them speak to students about drugs, assemblies, hiring, and the real world.

A loyal and active alumnus is an important asset and resource of your school, whether your building is elementary, middle, or high school. Invite former students to speak on whatever topic is relevant to the graduate: maybe they were Valedictorian for their year; maybe they started a successful company; or studied a year abroad; or pulled off a big fundraiser for the community.

Dr. Gilbert says, "Success breeds success," so take advantage of terrific graduates from recent years and let them be role models for the leaders of tomorrow.

Sometimes alumni can share less-than-exemplary stories that are just as helpful and inspiring to young listeners. Maybe they were arrested or are in recovery for drug addiction. These can be powerful messages that resonate because the presenter went to their school, sat in those same auditorium and classroom seats, and is not too much older than the current student body. If you are over 35, forget it. They look at us like old farts no matter what, so when you can set up a great alumni presentation with a powerful message, don't miss the chance.

60. Buy fundraising items from the school. Don't be cheap!

Chocolate, fruit, shirts, nuts, oh my! My rule is I'll buy one of everything. Yes, it adds up, and you feel like every time you turn around you are buying something else, but it is part of the job. PTSA selling umbrellas? Buy one. Senior class selling their grad shirt? Buy it. I recommend you write checks for these items and keep track, then claim them at tax time.

The kids and school groups appreciate (and expect!) your participation. Think about it: The 6th grade class is selling chocolate-covered almonds as a fundraiser for their end of the year trip, and the principal says "no" to buying a $9 bag because you've had enough of writing these checks . . .? How's that going to go over? Yes, you are right. Terribly. So suck it up and buy the stuff. It's part of the gig, and use the monies spent as write-offs on your taxes.

61. Wear school gear to school.

You are the leader and people will follow your lead. Buy a shirt with your school's logo and colors on it, and wear it to school!

We have fun with Port Pride Fridays at our school. Instead of teachers dressing down on Fridays, they wear all kinds of port gear. We've got everything you can think of: polo shirts, sweatshirts, tie-dye shirts, pullovers, and so on. It's great and everyone shows a lot of pride on these days.

62. Be strong on drugs, alcohol, and tobacco.

If you are in a middle school or high school, be tough on drugs and alcohol. If students are involved with these things, you and your school have to intervene asap, because it is a major problem for young people. If you look the other way or take a light stance, they could overrun your school.

Drugs are contagious. So is bad behavior. The students need to know that these issues will not be tolerated in the school and that they cannot get away with it. If students involved with drugs, alcohol, or tobacco are allowed to roam free and do as they please, they will share toxic items with countless students in your school.

You have a duty to your community, both the parents and young people in your school, to be tough on the bad temptations out there. The mind-set of: "I did it when I was young" or "It's not that bad" or "It's not heroin" is unacceptable. What seem like small issues or problems can very quickly turn into big problems for that kid and for your school. Nip it in the bud (no pun intended!). Discipline the student and get the parents involved. Bring in local agencies and get the affected students and families help. Throwing them out of school might make you feel tough, but getting them the appropriate help is really the most important thing and the noblest action on your part. Others might focus on the punishment/suspension, but getting them help is the best path toward the long-term goal vs. a temporary fix. Yes, they need to be punished accordingly if they are caught with banned substances, but you are dealing with teenagers. Whenever possible, focus on rehabilitation vs. punishment.

I recently caught a young lady drinking alcohol in school. She is a popular student-athlete. She received a 5-day suspension and a superintendent's hearing. I made part of her discipline to attend three AA meetings. I wanted her to hear alcoholics speak about their problems. I hoped the meetings would scare her and make her realize what she was doing was wrong. What's more impactful on a 14-year-old—a suspension where they sit at home playing video games, or looking into the eyes of a recovering alcoholic telling their story of struggles with sobriety? I had her write me a two-page report about what she learned, what her short-term goals were, and how she was going to change her ways. While some people in the school thought she should be suspended for one year, I decided this was the best solution for a young lady who had made a poor choice.

In every situation you think about all you've learned, what your mentors would do, and then follow your gut to do what you feel is best. Whatever you decide, the students and staff will know that you will not tolerate drugs/alcohol/tobacco in your school.

I had help with this idea from my brother-in-law, Ron Bentley. Ron is a police officer in New Canaan, CT, and a great one at that. He sees the ugly side of drugs and alcohol abuse when students continue to slide and he is arresting them a few years later. Having students caught with substances attend substance abuse meetings is proactive and shows a willingness to be flexible in your attempt to help. Great idea, Officer Bentley!

63. Don't hush-hush complicated episodes.

When you catch someone with drugs or a weapon, or you have a serious incident, you may feel the need to keep it quiet. I am of the opposite thought—get it out there. If there is a problem, you need to make it public and get others' attention. Yes, there is negative publicity, but you can deal with that by meeting it head on.

Be strong and vigilant. Stand up at school board meetings, school assemblies, PTSA meetings, and faculty meetings. Talk about the issues and how you are going to attack each problem. Offer solutions and ideas for how you plan to make it better. You're not bringing the drugs into the school, but you are the principal, so it is your problem. Take care of it. Open it up and get after it.

One of the first things I was proud to accomplish at Port Jervis was attacking the smoking problem. I remember when I first walked into the school for my interview, I smelled smoke right away. Students and staff smoked in our building like they were getting paid for it. It was just outside every back door, and forget even trying to go in the bathrooms. You needed a fan just to clear the air and see where you were going. There were cigarettes and cigarette butts everywhere. I said to myself: We cannot have this where people are trying to work and learn.

I hooked up with a local health agency that had a grant to work specifically with schools. I was able to get some free pens, pencils, and a huge banner for the school front that read, "Proud to Be Smoke Free." Instead of hanging up signs that said Don't Smoke as a reprimand, I wanted to be positive and proactive. We started the slogan: PJ Proud to Be Smoke Free and put it everywhere. The district backed me, and I was able to order signage that we put all over the school. Through the grant I was able to purchase smoke detectors that had beepers. The detectors were put in the bathrooms, and when there was smoke from a cigarette, our beepers beeped and we were there in seconds. Bam. The problem was eradicated within a few weeks. No more cigarette butts, no more smell, no more smoking in our school. It worked great and we haven't had that problem again.

FIGURE 3.1 "Smoke & minors," article by Ashley Kelly for *The Times Herald-Record*. Used with permission.

Times Herald-Record Wednesday, August 29, 2007

Inmates suing for religious books

By Oliver Mackson
Times Herald-Record
omackson@th-record.com

Otisville – On behalf of federal prison inmates across the country, Moshe Milstein is hoping to make a federal case over Maimonides, the Rev. Rick Warren and other spiritual scribes.

Milstein and another inmate at the Otisville Federal Prison Camp last week filed a class-action federal lawsuit against the U.S. Bureau of Prisons. They contend that the feds violated inmates' constitutional rights of religious freedom and due process by restricting access to religious books.

Milstein, 61, was released from Otisville to a halfway house yesterday after serving a sentence for fraud involving mislabeled prescription drugs.

One of his lawyers, Moses Silverman of New York City, said that Milstein isn't looking for a payday. He's going to court because the Bureau of Prisons enacted a policy earlier this year that limits the number of religious books for each faith available in prison chapels.

"This is not a suit for damages. It's a suit to deal with what we consider the important issue of access to religious freedom and access to religious materials in prison," Silverman said.

Milstein, an Orthodox Jew, is one of two Otisville inmates suing. The other, John J. Okon, is a Christian. They sued over the book policy earlier this year but dropped it after a judge urged them to go through the prison's administrative process.

> **MOSHE MILSTEIN, AN ORTHODOX JEW, IS ONE OF TWO OTISVILLE INMATES SUING. THE OTHER, JOHN J. OKON, IS A CHRISTIAN.**

The lawsuit describes that effort as a bureaucratic dead end. So Milstein and Okon went back to court.

A Bureau of Prisons spokeswoman couldn't be reached yesterday, but the agency's position was outlined earlier this summer by a federal prosecutor after the three inmates first sued.

The prosecutor, Briand Feldman, told the judge that the dispute grew out of a 2004 Department of Justice review of how prisons choose the providers of Muslim religious services.

Feldman told the judge that the Justice Department review was done because of concern that prisons "had been radicalized by inmates who were practicing or espousing various extreme forms of religion, specifically Islam, which exposed security risks to the prisons and beyond the prisons to the public at large."

Silverman says the feds haven't explained why Warren's "The Purpose-Driven Life" or books by the 12th-century Jewish sage Maimonides are security problems.

"Frankly, I think the Bureau of Prisons policy here is incomprehensible," Silverman said. "I would think people of all political persuasions, from the right to the left, the left to the right, would agree that having people have access to religious literature would be a good thing."

Times Herald-Record photos/CHET GORDON
Joe Riordan, left, owner of the Try-R-Deli in Deerpark, talks yesterday with Andrew Marotta, assistant principal at Port Jervis High School. Marotta has persuaded three local businesses, including the deli, to remove their smoking advertisements.

Official gets shops to ax cigarette ads

By Ashley Kelly
Times Herald-Record
akelly@th-record.com

Deerpark – Andrew Marotta's message is clear: Port Jervis High School is smoke-free.

For the past year, Marotta, an assistant principal at the high school, has spread the nonsmoking message by posting signs throughout the campus and warning students of the dangers of smoking.

But this summer, he took it a step further by persuading three local businesses to sign an agreement to reduce or eliminate cigarette ads in their stores.

Marotta hopes the decrease in signs will deter students from buying cigarettes.

When Marotta began working at the high school three years ago, he noticed the smell of smoke coming from the bathrooms.

What is this, kids smoking here? Marotta thought. "I had to do something."

Marotta reached out to the anti-smoking coalition POW'R (Putnam, Orange, Westchester, Rockland) Against Tobacco. With grant money from the coalition, Marotta has been able to buy smoke-free signs, smoke detectors and a huge smoke-free banner that is on display at the entrance of the school.

When Marotta asked

Assistant Principal Andrew Marotta poses yesterday with Port Jervis High School's new smoke-free emblem on the gym floor.

store owners Bill and Vicky Harris to participate in the school's no-smoking effort, it was a no-brainer. The couple owns Traditions Olde Country Store & Deli on Route 42.

The Harrises said they don't sell cigarettes by the carton or offer discounts for cigarettes.

"We don't need to advertise that we have cigarettes," said Bill Harris, who quit smoking

more than a year ago. "People know we have them."

Try-R-Deli on Route 209 in Deerpark and the Daily Stop on Jersey Avenue in Port Jervis also have signed the agreement to limit cigarette ads.

Students from the school's Tobacco Free School group will continue to ask local businesses to sign the agreement this year.

Punishment for smoking at the high school is a one-day suspension for the first offense and two days' suspension for a second offense.

Meghan DuBois, of Orange County coalition coordinator for POW'R Against Tobacco, said many teens don't realize that tobacco companies are using them to make a profit.

"What he's doing is off the charts," said DuBois, referring to Marotta's work. "He's appealing to potential replacement smokers whom the companies are trying to attract."

DuBois said replacement smokers are new smokers who take the place of people who have died from smoking-related illness or people who quit.

"I want students to be proud to not do it – not that you're a nerd because you don't smoke," Marotta said.

Any businesses in the Port Jervis area that would like to get involved should call Andrew Marotta at 856-3110.

FIGURE 3.2 "Official gets shops to ax cigarette ads," article by Ashley Kelly for *The Times Herald-Record*. Used with permission.

64. Set up a see something, say something culture.

I grew up in NYC and was teaching when 9/11 happened. I watched from the roof of my school in Staten Island as the Towers burned and fell. I remember the black smoke and smell vividly. When I arrived in upstate NY as assistant principal and now principal, I brought former NYC Mayor Rudy Giuliani's saying and safety philosophy with me: "See something, say something."

Cultivate a culture where students and staff feel comfortable letting those in charge know if something is wrong. Give people avenues to reach you without them being noticed. People want good and truth in the world, and when something is wrong, their voices should be heard: by you! Make this part of your leadership philosophy. In addition to making school safer, it will help you with parents and the community. They will feel comforted that you are willing and want to listen. Put it on signs, put it in your school letters, say it on the loudspeaker, and tell students in assemblies. If you listen, they will talk. People will step forward and stop evil from occurring in your building on your watch.

65. Graduation: Managing major moments!

Kindergarten, fifth grade, moving up to eighth grade, and then high school. It does not matter what level, they are all important, milestone ceremonies. As I state many times in this book, you are in charge and 100% responsible for making these ceremonies great. Grandmas, grandpas, aunts, uncles, and so on, are all there in the house to celebrate the graduation of their child. They expect it to be beautiful, memorable, and perfect, and it is on you to make that happen.

We've already covered many things that support the graduation event development process. Hold meetings to plan in advance, be prepared, be transparent and clear with all information and communication. Ensure that the area is clean, prepped, looking fabulous, and ready for the crowds that will attend.

I adopted this tip about managing major moments from the former NCAA Director of Officiating, John Adams. As a school principal, graduation is one of, if not the biggest, thing required of you. This is a chance for you, your school, and your whole program to shine on the biggest stage. You want to knock graduation out of the park.

Here are a few more graduation planning tips that may or may not be new to you. If you don't already use them, put these in place asap:

- Start planning early, especially if this is your first or second time.
- Make a checklist with due dates and responsible parties.
- What is your rain plan? Emergency plan?
- Do you have enough handicapped seating? A lot of elderly people attend graduation.
- Create a map and put everything you want on there, showing its intended place. (Including a flag on the stage! Take a guess why I'm reminding you of this!)
- Have the map at the meeting for all parties to review, and go over it with the students as well.
- Meet with the students and tell them your expectations of a respectful and classy ceremony. Be bold and direct with them.
- Hold a brainstorming session with your cabinet and have the "what if" situations discussion. Be ready for everything.
- Make your speech awesome—write it like a comet: memorable, brilliant, and brief.
- Double check lighting, batteries, and shine your shoes.

- Have the grass cut two days before.
- Check the weather five days out and then each day afterward.
- Take a deep breath and do a good job. Period.
- Keep a clipboard with you on stage and in real time, and write down things you want to change about the ceremony for the future.

66. Collect tribute letters.

As graduation ceremony approaches and you are preparing, send out a notice to parents and loved ones, requesting tribute letters for your students. Tribute letters are written to the student from parents, grandparents, brothers and sisters, godparents, and so on, at the time of their special graduation. I like to give them out when the students receive their caps, gowns, and yearbooks. It is a special time for students to receive a warm and loving message from a family member or close friend. Good times for all, so even though it is already packed, add this to your end-of-the-year schedule. Most students' families will enjoy writing them and the students love reading them; but keep in mind that not every student comes from a loving, supportive family. Make sure that for any children who do not have relatives attending or cheering their graduation, you and your staff write personal, handwritten notes for those kids, letting them know how proud you are that they have made it all the way to the big day. Trust me, it will not be lost on them. I sincerely hope you will embrace and employ every one of the tips in this book over time, and this one is super special. Make it happen!

67. Hang up the yearly staff picture.

If this is already a tradition at your school, keep it going. If it's not, make it one. Set it up with the company that takes student photos.

Having staff pics hung in the hall is an absolute sign of respect for the teachers in the school, acknowledging their giant part in the school's success. Students, parents, and the staff themselves see the pictures, and it is another way to bring your community together. A photo of all of the professionals, including clerical and support staff, should hang proudly on the wall. It is a nice thing that you can do for your school. Once photos are there three or four years in a row, it is cool to see all the new faces and reminisce about the ones who have left your staff. My superintendent, Mr. B, always says the staff you leave with in June is the not the same group that returns in September. Get a nice 11 x 14 picture hung up! Include your theme for the year in the photo. The company can print the theme right into the picture. If not, get a cheap label maker, write the annual theme, and stick it on the frame. People will identify the theme with the year and think back to it and the good times from that school year.

68. Eat in the café with the kids.

A delicious, juicy steak; a fine glass of wine; smooth jazz playing in the background . . . a relaxing, peaceful atmosphere. A picturesque view of the city . . . not! That's not exactly how you will spend lunch hours in school. My advice to you is to have lunch with the students in the café at least two or three times a week. Those beautiful, relaxing meals described above will be for another time, but not while you're on the job. Get with the kids. Let them see you as a person, not only a principal. Laugh with them, ask them their favorite tv shows, if they watched the game last night, and what did they think about the election? Where are they going to go to college; if they had a million dollars, where would they go and what would they do with it? You get the point.

Your time is limited and precious, so spend it wisely. Eating in the café gets you a number of things: You get to eat! Your people see you, both staff and students. You are helping to supervise a large number of students where you are always only one McNugget away from a food fight. You get to talk to students in a nonacademic setting, and you get to be out of your office . . . all very important. Add eating in the café with the kids to your schedule. Make it happen.

4

Work With the Adults

Engage Staff and Parents to Strengthen Your School Community

69. Be relentless in having your staff keep in contact with parents.

Many schools have no requirement for teachers to call parents. Some find it easy; it comes naturally. Other teachers can be hesitant and even afraid of some conflict on the other end of the line, so they prefer to use e-mail or stick to the old-fashioned report card or progress report.

It is essential for you to keep on teachers to call parents. A face-to-face conversation is probably best, but unless that parent comes in, you have to settle for a phone call. Be relentless on this issue because if you are not, it is human nature to settle for what is most comfortable, and some teachers will not keep up with parents the way they need to.

Calling parents involves some skill, and tips for these exchanges include finding something positive to say, listening until the parent is completely done speaking, communicating a student's shortcomings without offending the parent, and so on. Each personal call is crucial. Encourage direct contact with parents—talk about it often. Although in most cases you cannot contractually insist that teachers do this, make it clear that it is of supreme importance to the school community you are trying to develop and reinforce.

When there is a particular issue with a student, you can follow up with the parents afterwards, but let the teacher make first contact, and always support your staff. Make sure they know you have their backs.

70. Update phone numbers constantly.

Make sure you have a system in place so people can easily update phone numbers. Don't leave room for excuses that "All the numbers don't work" or "I can't get in touch with parents if the numbers are not accurate." This is a small fix, but a big one. Get on it. Make it easy to call students' homes by looking up school numbers with a simple click.

How are your school contact numbers changed and updated now? Do systems with necessary info talk to one another? Nurse, transportation, food services, and so on . . . are they all housed under one roof? Check it out and make it a simple process for all parties to cross-reference for easy access to help.

71. Nominate people for awards to celebrate your staff.

This is one of the fun parts of the job. Celebrating the people in your school or district is a great thing you can do for all stakeholders in your school. A few years into my position as AP, John Xanthis nominated me for a prestigious county award for excellence. It was a great evening with family and friends attending, and I felt very proud to have been nominated. I still have the plaque on my wall today.

I learned from that experience that it is good to nominate people for awards. A custodian, your assistant principal, a top teacher, a secretary.

We've had two great award experiences during my time at PJHS:

First, Heidi Nyland, our superstar assistant principal, won NYS Assistant Principal in 2014. She is a strong woman with a big heart for students. She deserved the award for going all out for our students and school. I nominated her with enthusiastic support from a number of our teachers and the superintendent, and she won! It was a great celebration for Heidi and for our school.

FIGURE 4.1

FIGURE 4.2

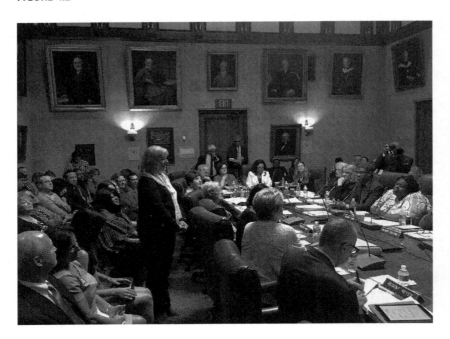

FIGURE 4.3

Our second nominee was Carolyn Dorritie—warm, friendly, dedicated, and one of our most dynamic teachers. Carolyn is highly intelligent, super kind, and has a special way of actually making kids like math. She is amazing. I nominated her for NYS Teacher of the Year, and Carolyn embraced the process. She made it all the way to the final five and landed in the top three. We celebrated her accomplishments each step of the way to the final ceremony. We used twitter posts, e-mail blasts, announcements at BOE meetings, school announcements, classroom parties, and so on, throughout the process. We swung for the fence and just missed, but it was a wonderful experience for Carolyn and for our district. We view her as our Teacher of the Year, and I am thrilled we did it.

Look for these opportunities and pick a deserving person. It is a little more work for you as principal, but a win all the way around. The person who is nominated feels good, you feel good for writing the nomination, and it elevates the school climate. Spread the love!

72. Let the air out of the balloon.

Talking to upset parents or staff members can be a challenge. People come at you, and when it is their children or their work, causes they are passionate about, it can be a lot of emotional energy to manage. Your first instinct might be to respond and defend yourself, but it is really important to let them have their say. I call it "letting the air out of the ominous balloon."

Imagine the image of a balloon in the chair in front of you in your office, ready to burst. If you put any pressure on it, especially something sharp, it will pop instantly, loudly, and then deflate. Explosions are not what you want in your office.

What does that parent or staff member want? They want to be heard. They need to be acknowledged and validated. Do that. Give them an attentive, understanding audience. Let all the air out of the balloon, whether they are in your office or on the phone. Be an active listener and take notes, so you can respond when it is your turn. Use words and phrases like: Go on, I hear you; I'm listening; I understand; and so on.

Ask the question, "Is there anything else?" and then repeat their concerns in recap to make sure you are on the same page with them. Say, "So I'd like to review your concerns, to make sure I get it right." Then go through each one.

Even if you don't agree, even if they are way off base or out in left field, let them finish. Don't get me wrong here, you are not a doormat, nor should you allow people to walk over you. You will soon see that being an active listener calms the other person, puts them at ease, and assures them that you care, which helps them let their guard down and puts you in control of the situation.

You are going to have many conflicts to resolve, and a revolving door of upset parents and staff members, so work at this. It is a skill developed over time for most, with a select few having the gift to swiftly and easily resolve conflicts.

73. Do not let parents curse at you or be disrespectful.

If a parent or guardian is being belligerent and/or swearing at you, interrupt them and say in a firm voice, "If you continue to curse rather than speak respectfully, I am ending this meeting (or call)." If they do it again, tell them again why you are hanging up and hang up the phone, or stand and open your office door to end the meeting. You can easily defend that action. You do not have to accept or tolerate abusive language. If they are making an outrageous accusation against you, firmly but calmly cut them off again, and do not entertain any nonsense. You are there to listen and hear their concerns, not take a verbal beating. Be clear on the difference. It is okay to demand/expect anyone in your office to honor reasonable behavior boundaries.

74. Be fast and firm with discipline.

Whether you are in a 200-student elementary school or a high school of 4,000, you need to follow strong, consistent discipline. Be swift, quick, and fair. Don't hesitate or shy away from enforcing the rules.

Yes, you will encounter parents who may be angry with you and blame you because their child punched the window out. Just remind yourself and your APs that "you did not do anything wrong." Your job is to manage each situation and give a fair, appropriate consequence for bad choices. Instill the values you want to maintain in your school by enforcing consistent rules that guide staff and student behavior.

Remember that each and every incident is different, and must be viewed as such. Yes, there is such a thing as precedent, but each incident has its own set of circumstances. A boy who brings a knife to school and who threatened a student one day before is different from an Eagle Scout student who is going to a project after school and had a knife included with his supplies in his bag.

Use your experience, common sense, and poise as an educational leader to make the hard decisions.

75. Explain and maintain that your focus is on correcting unacceptable behavior patterns and setting students on the right path, not punishment.

Many parents and teachers get caught up in the appropriate punishment for something vs. if the administration's actions helped to fix the behavior. Some want a pound of flesh for a simple crime, and it is your job to weigh all factors in the situation to make the wise, fair call, even when it is not popular.

Focus on correcting unacceptable behaviors or decision patterns, not the consequence. One student—we'll call her TJ—was an excitable freshman who made a poor decision. She pranked the county suicide prevention hotline. After some legwork, we found out it was her and she admitted to doing it. She received a shorter suspension than we may normally have given her; but as part of the punishment, she had to apologize to the school where she told the hotline she was a student (after which the hotline frantically spent about three to four hours trying to locate this fake student). She also had to apologize to the suicide hotline staff.

This is another recommendation from Office Ron Bentley, my brother-in-law, a decorated and beloved police officer in New Canaan, CT. Instead of quickly locking young people up, Ron has developed a technique of matching the right punishment (outside the box) for each situation. Rather than simply making someone pay a fine or get a bad charge on their record that will hurt them later in life, Ron's suggested response in this situation made sense, and I was pleased with the outcome.

This young lady did not realize the serious repercussions of her actions when she made that call, so my first goal was to make her realize what she did was wrong. She and her mom both thanked me for having her go to the school and the suicide hotline office. It helped her to see and face the people who were affected and had to deal with her actions in the moment. This was a good example of keeping focus on correcting the unacceptable behavior and poor decision making vs. caring only about the punishment.

76. Do not wait until the last year of a teacher's tenure application if you do not believe they will earn tenure.

Granting tenure is like a marriage. You most likely are going to be with that person forever, so you need to make good decisions with tenure, and you do not want to wait until the final year of their application cycle. I have written for you to be patient, to give people chances, and you must also set a timeline. If tenure in your district is three years, you really have one year to get a feel and make up your mind about them. If it is four years, you have two years. Get in that person's class.

Invite them to lunch. Do the walk and talk. Put the time into getting to know them so you are ready when the time comes. Get a feel for each tenure candidate early, and gather the info you need to make appropriate choices for your school.

77. In select cases, grant a jewel year.

If you are struggling with a decision about tenure for a teacher or employee, your best answer is probably not to grant tenure. You do have another choice, though, and that is a jewel year.

A jewel is an extension of the tenure period, usually up to one year. If you do grant a jewel, you must be clear and specific about the measurable criteria the teacher must improve on. Meet with them and the union. Be clear, so there are no surprises. They either comply with required improvements and make it or they don't, but you gave them an extra chance and time to achieve success.

78. Ask parents: What do you think is fair?

When parents come in to see you, ask them, "How can I help you? What can I do for you? If you were the principal, what do you think is a fair punishment?"

For the most part, people don't go to see the principal unless they have a reason, so get to it. "How can I help you?" And when you've asked them how you can help, don't forget to listen to their answer. Let them get all the air out of their balloon. Listen until they are finished. Sometimes they just want to get something off their chest, or maybe they have a specific request. After doing this for so many years, I've heard it all.

As principal you have a super-full plate to manage each day, but experience over time will help you build confidence until you feel prepared for any incident or challenge.

79. Make faculty meetings short, productive, and engaging.

You have ten a year, maybe eleven. These are your lesson plans. You expect teachers to have great, engaging lessons to keep students learning, and the same goes for you. Make faculty meetings informative, interactive, and fun. The staff is tired and doesn't want to be there in the first place, so make it work for them. Be quick but not in a hurry, and professional but not too serious. It is all about balance.

I'm a fan of finding something positive to share with the staff, celebrating births and milestones, and telling funny or crowd-pleasing stories, themed under, "Did that really happen?" I also like, "Did you know?"—where you can share something interesting about a staff member that maybe people did not know.

On my staff we have people who are master cake chefs, or rode cross country on a motorcycle, and one person who wore a different shirt for 112 consecutive days of school (no, I am not making this up!). You can give them all the necessary dates and information required during the meeting, but it will always be the stories that sell. Work on your plan and make each meeting great.

80. Inspect what you expect. Stand by your demands.

If you have expectations for certain things in your building (as principal, you better!), then you need to inspect what you expect. Teachers in the hallways at the bell, sitting in the first ten rows at faculty meetings, staff to attend certain night events. . . . When you have an expectation, you need to inspect during events to make sure what you requested is happening.

I learned this from my friend, Dr. Deanna Stevenson, through our professional development sessions with PLC Associates. I am often reminded that this "ain't" my dad's pharmacy. In the old days in Staten Island, if there was a problem with someone or something in Dad's small place of business, he could very easily just let the person go. He had some people move on, but mostly worked with a small number of people over the life of the pharmacy.

After selling the pharmacy, my dad joined Walgreens for a number of years. He was the head pharmacist, supervising others while training interns and students. Once there was a young man who did not like to shave. My father explained about looking professional and the importance of looking clean-cut and clean-shaven each day. The young man did not take too well to what my dad told him was expected of him. The next day he did not shave and began his shift. My father addressed him sternly, asking if he wanted to work there and be part of the team. The young man responded with a resounding yes. Dad said, "Then here's what you have to do. Go sign out of the store, buy a razor and shave cream from the store, go to the bathroom and shave, and then sign back in, and do not come to work unshaven again." That was the end of it. The young employee did as he was told, and they actually went on to become friends, mentor and mentee, in a father/son-like relationship. The young man eventually invited my folks to his wedding, and toasted my father at the ceremony, saying to the room, "Thank you to Mr. Joe, for teaching me to become a pharmacist and a man." When you follow through on your expectations, not only are you making sure demands are met, but you also show your staff that they need to take you and themselves seriously. Requests need to be clear, with measurable results. Inspect what you expect!

81. Develop a good working relationship with your teachers' union.

This can be crucial to your success. Every school is different, each with its own culture, a set of values and energy in the working relationship. For some reason there are teachers (not all!) who have an "us vs. them" mentality. They seem to work against you and every goal you try to accomplish.

Get to a good working relationship with the union. Be respectful of them, not a pushover. Meet with them. Encourage communication and set an example for it. The contract is a funny thing. Some people couldn't care less about it while others live and die by it. Some walk out of work each day at 2:30 p.m. on the dot because that's what the contract says. Some show up to work right at 7:30 a.m. because that's what their contract lists as required. Like I mentioned in an earlier point of wisdom, have a loose and tight mentality. Pick and choose your battles carefully.

82. Get rid of bad employees.

After you have counseled them, warned them, and met with their union reps . . . after you have tried to cover for them, written them up, and given them extra chances . . . after you have tried all these things and more, it is time for them to go.

It is very difficult in the world of education to remove employees from their job, even when they are awful. There are many rules in place that protect grown-ups without considering the negative impact on the children when bad people are saved by the system. I am amazed in today's advanced society that we still have some of these archaic rules in place, but they are there, and you need to know how to navigate your work in spite of them.

Tony DiMarco, who hired me, told me, "There are only two things you can do to significantly improve your school, especially when it comes to personnel. Either make the people you have better, or get better people." I write about both in this book, and getting better people isn't the hard part. The hurdle is getting rid of staff members who aren't cutting it.

You already know that I believe in giving people chances, and I understand that embracing all different types is not only what makes the world go 'round, but also makes for good schools. What I have little to zero tolerance for is adults who hurt kids—mentally, physically, or educationally.

Teachers who play head games with students better fix whatever their issue is, or they will get my attention quickly. Do not hurt kids. Period. As the school's leader, pay close attention to anyone in or around a situation where an adult is negatively affecting a student; and when the only option is to fire that person, here are a few tips to make it easier:

◆ Make sure you are in the person's room often. Do several walk-throughs and formal observations.

◆ Send a second or third set of eyes in as well: send your APs.

◆ Document what you see in the class and any complaints from parents or students.

◆ Let the person know through a meeting with a union rep what your concerns are. Be specific with dates, times, and actions/words by that employee. Take meticulous notes.

◆ If the issue continues, write the person up. Hold another union meeting; be perfectly clear and specific in your report. Reference any previous meetings that you have had with the person and what was addressed in those meetings.

◆ Be prepared. If they are violating any specific policies, state the policy, policy number, and where it is written. Make sure to follow all rules/procedures about putting the complaint letter or report in the person's file. Double check to be certain it gets in there.

◆ Continue to monitor the behavior and document everything in factual detail: dates, times, words/actions, and so on.

Yes, this is another layer of the job that sometimes creates extra work for you, but you cannot ignore a problem staff member. It is important first and foremost to live by the code of treating every kid as if they were your own kid and would you want your own child in this person's class? If the answer after all attempts at observation, counseling, guidance, warning, and write-up is still no, then you must do something about it. While it is highly important to have your staff's backs, don't let that cloud your judgment when a situation needs correction. You can't ever lose sight of putting the kids first. Student safety and providing a comfortable, encouraging learning environment are your top priorities.

5

Get Organized and Always Be Prepared

83. Keep a notepad with you at all times.

As principal, you are a busy person. This cannot be overstated; there is a lot happening at all times. Your list of things that you need to do, take care of, prepare for, and so on, is always growing and changing. Keep a notepad with you at all times and jot down everything you need to remember. If you are a tech person and prefer to use your smartphone digital notepad, do it.

Use any tools available to create, modify, check off, and add to your ever-changing and growing to-do list. I use a 5" × 7" notepad that I can tuck in the back of my pants or easily carry with me. I go through nearly a pad a week taking down thoughts, tasks, and reminders. I write my daily task chart on there and then look back at it throughout each day to see what I can cross off and what needs to roll over to the next day.

84. Do what you say you are going to do.

Very important. Very important! You are always being watched and evaluated, and you do not want people thinking/saying that you do not keep your word. So if you say it, you have to do it. You can change your mind. You aren't necessarily locked into everything you discuss with others, but for the most part, say what you mean and mean what you say. You'll earn trust as people discover that you honor your word.

Be mindful of what you say. Use your notepad or ask Siri to remind you, but don't make promises and then forget. I ask people to hold on—"Let me write that down, because if I do not write it down I may not remember." It's okay to be honest. People know you're busy.

Beyond notepad and smartphone or tablet, you can rely on your secretary to help you. Post-its, taped notes, electronic reminders . . . with all these options you can develop a system that works for you and makes things happen.

85. Don't take calls from angry parents.

Nothing good comes from speaking with an angry temper. Have your secretary take a message. Give them time to cool off.

If it is pertinent, briefly take the call and tell them you will call them back within 24 hours. You will get angry parents from time to time; hopefully not too often, but they do call. Trust me, do not take those calls. They want a piece of you at that moment; do not give it to them. Once they have some time to cool off you can get back to them, and make sure you do. You'll be in more hot water if you don't reach them promptly.

When you do return a phone call, if they do not pick up, make sure you leave a message and write down the date and time. Keep a record of everything so you can easily look back without having to remember.

I once had a very angry parent who just wanted to argue with me. I listened. I followed many of the tips and wisdom points in this book (air out of the balloon, stay calm, etc.), but this father would not stop. Any time he paused I would ask, "Sir, may I respond?"

"Go ahead!" he'd yell, but as I would attempt to answer, he would interrupt me and start talking loudly again. I finally said that if he would not let me speak, I was hanging up, and as he continued to yell, that is just what I did.

Well . . . that led to a call to the superintendent, who then called me. I advised him to not call the parent back that day, to wait until the next day, but he got stuck in a long, one-way tirade from this parent that went very similar to mine—nothing productive, a waste of time. The superintendent ended his call prematurely as well, because that parent was not able to listen or hear any attempt to resolve the matter. It is almost always best to wait a day rather than take calls from angry people.

86. Have your script ready.

You meet with a lot people and do a lot of talking throughout the day. When you have a formal presentation, have your notes ready to make sure you hit all the key points. With so much happening each day and so many things racing through your mind, take five minutes before your meeting starts to write down bullet points of what you want to say. This is a small thing to do that has a major impact on keeping prepared, calm, and confident.

87. Give the person(s) you are meeting with a copy of your talking points.

The person might not be an auditory learner. A list of your speaking points will help them follow along and pay attention because they have the notes in front of them. They will also have a written record of your points after you are finished. Try it. It supports the goals of clarity and transparency.

Note: I don't do this for every meeting. I carefully choose when it will be helpful and appropriate. It removes the element of surprise, and if the person is upset or angry during the meeting, they can look back and review the material when they have calmed down.

88. Take care of items and issues for the superintendent right away.

The superintendents are your bosses. You cannot miss their stuff: replying to e-mails, attending meetings, dealing with things, and so on. In spite of whatever is flying at you, make sure you see and tend to your bosses' stuff. Put it on your to-do list. When they call, e-mail, text, and so on, get right to it and get back to them promptly. You do not want to be a complicator. Be a simplifier. This is from my officiating boss, John Clougherty.

John was a great college basketball official, working twelve Final Fours. He then took over the ACC and hired me on the staff. He always told us to be a simplifier, not a complicator. The bosses have a lot going on and a lot on their plate. You do not want to add to that by giving them any reason to worry about you: Are you going to show? Will you complete the task? Will you have your presentation ready? If you miss a couple of times, they will start to doubt you and not trust you. Not good! If you are not tenured, you can forget it. You'll be out quickly.

89. Plan ahead for next year—brainstorm, write it down, build a budget.

Despite a hectic pace in the halls each day, making change happen in a school is not a fast thing. Sometimes you can change or fix something easily, but most efforts take at least a year to execute, especially if you need to buy something. Keep a running list of important items you need to purchase, how those expenditures relate to goals you want to accomplish, and things you'd like to change.

It's hard to accomplish things when the train is moving. It takes a while to change course during the school year. Minor adjustments are not necessarily a big deal, but for brand-new things, wait for the ship to dock for summer. During the summer, everybody is reloading, refreshing, and getting ready for the new year. There is an expectation of new initiatives and new ideas when teachers return, so plan ahead and develop a budget. If you do not have a budget allocated for it, more often than not, you can't buy it.

90. Know the teachers' contract. Know the law and the rules.

There is no excuse for not being up to speed on these items. Ask questions, read books, network with peers and get in the know. When people disagree with you on issues, just follow the contract; you can't go wrong. When I referee my college hoops games and a coach questions me or one of my calls, I try to answer most times with, "By rule . . . " When I can answer in that manner, there is not much they can say in response. It is essential and enormously helpful to know the rules. The same goes for school.

I try very hard not to live and die by the contract, but it is important that you know the contract, along with its ins and outs. There are things in there you need to be aware of, and things that happen in your building that are openly accepted although not necessarily in the contract. Why is that? Why is that allowed? The words "past practice" get thrown around a lot. My advice is to know the contract as well as you can without being a lawyer. Read it. Keep a copy in your desk. Refer to it. Quote it.

Years ago, I wanted to get rid of our old-fashioned waste of time study halls and replace them with a more pro-active, engaging, guided learning model—a period where the teacher actively works with students in the subject area in which they are failing. Teachers were not used to this change, nor were they ready for it. The contract read that teachers can give AIS (academic intervention service) to students every other day, but this clause in the contract had never been used. Teachers used to have non-academic duties like hall duty, café duty, and other non-teaching obligations. I proposed to change all of the other responsibilities to guided learning sessions, where teachers would engage and challenge struggling students. This was a fight but it was in the contract, and this was one of the changes that helped us increase our graduation rate from 61% to 84.7% over ten years. The change was not welcome or easy; it was hard work, but ultimately, we were able to make it happen. This was a great thing for our students, but it would not have been possible if that clause had not been in the contract.

91. Follow up on what you see.

A cracked floor tile, a teacher showing up late, a parent berating an official at a sporting event, a student speeding in town . . . follow up on what you see. I repeatedly suggest keeping a notepad with you at all times. Whether print or digital, write down everything that comes your way. Your ever-changing and growing to-do list should include following up on anything that needs to be addressed in your school community. Often these follow-ups may happen organically with little effort; but you must not forget, ignore, or neglect things, so keep that list close, flexible, and current at all times.

92. Mix up your routine every once in a while.

It is easy to get into an ironclad pattern. The bells, the days, the lunches. My wife calls it the rut. Mix it up every once in a while. If you greet students at the front door every day, go outside to the corner one day. If you usually go to 4th period lunch, go to 5th one day. You'll see different things, people, and might even catch some things people did not want you to see, because they weren't expecting you in that spot. Try it. You may like it. Put a reminder in your schedule to get to a different spot once or twice a week.

When I first became principal, we had some terrible occurrences in the parking lot. I have different monitors and security people walk through there to show a presence, and I decided that I needed to see what the heck was going on for myself; so one day I jumped in my car and just sat there, parked. I faced out so I could see and the students could see me. Another day I parked and sat right in the middle of the lot. Students were looking at me like I was crazy—what is he doing here? The next day I parked at the entrance, and the fourth day I was standing near the crosswalk. One student walked by shaking his head. He said, "Man, you are everywhere!" That made me feel good about my decision to mix it up, let the students know I am always right there, visible, out in the open. I care what is happening in the parking lot. I'm paying attention.

93. Know where all teachers and personnel are at all times.

It can be on your phone, tablet, memorized, in your planner, or like I have, on a folded, laminated paper tucked into the back of my pants (my partners call them my butt papers). These papers are the schedules of every staff member in the building. I know where they all are at all times. If I need something or someone, I can get them within seconds. Format doesn't matter, just have everyone's schedule with you at all times. This shows organization, preparedness, and leadership. The captain of the ship knows where all crew members are at all times.

94. Take good notes.

Your notebook will get subpoenaed. At some point, whether or not it is the superintendent in a discipline hearing or a lawyer in an accident case, your notes will be read and examined. So take great notes and learn how to do it quickly. Listen carefully, write fast, and ask the correct questions. I certainly would advise for new principals (and APs) to go to training on how to question witnesses to incidents. Here are a couple of pointers to get you started:

- Write down the date and time when you interview the person(s).
- Try to have someone with you when you conduct interviews, especially if it is sensitive or sexual in nature. Preferably an assistant principal if you have one.
- Get the scene: Where exactly were you sitting? Who was sitting next to you? Around you? Draw a sketch or map of the scene.
- What exactly did they say? Be specific. Get the words, did they yell it, whisper it? How did they hit the person? Closed fist, open-handed slap? Proximity . . . you get the idea. The devil is in the details. Be as precise as possible.
- Use the scale of one to ten: Ten is a knockout punch; one is a light tap with one finger. Ten is the loudest yell or scream you ever heard; and one is a whisper from a grandma in church. The right questions and detailed answers will help you get a better idea of what happened and how it happened.
- Make a list of witnesses and a schedule to interview them.
- Write down any other notes regarding the incident that you think would be helpful. (i.e., The students were nervous and sweaty when I spoke to them. They were all over the place while answering and changed their story three times.)

- Write down the date and time you contact parents, the police, and so on.
- Make sure you follow any rules about child abuse reporting or child protective services. If you are not sure, ask someone. If you can't get in touch with someone, err on the side of making the call.
- Write down the order of actions taken when you found out _____. Conduct a headline test (see Tip 14).

Record everything you do from the moment you find out. Simply put, take good notes. It can and will help you if and when they ever get examined.

95. Date the front of each notebook.

Write down on the cover of your notebook the day you started using it and the day you finished. That way you can always look back to your notes from a certain time frame if you need to find something. Date each page and keep the old books in a file for easy reference if you need them. You never know.

6

Plan and Execute Meetings for Comfort and Productivity

96. Do the DiMarco. Start with the end and then rewind.

As principal, your days (and sometimes nights, too) are an endless run of meetings and conversations with people: staff, parents, students, guests, new hires, and so on. When the stakes are high, get right to the point. We call this "the DiMarco," named after Tony DiMarco. Don't keep people holding their breath. Start with the news, whatever the topic is, and then go back to explain the details. "I am not hiring you for this position . . . You are being suspended for five days . . . I am going to grant you this leave of absence . . . " are a few examples of high-stakes situations where your audience is heavily waiting on your decision. Look them in the eye, get it out there, and then go back and explain, listen to their questions, and so on. I compare it to ripping off the Band-Aid. It may hurt for a few seconds, but it is over and done.

97. Meeting before the meeting . . . shirt before the shirt.

In the early 2000s there was a big hit MTV show, *Jersey Shore*. It was like a car wreck that you could not turn away from. Yes, I am guilty; I actually watched it from time to time. Growing up in Staten Island, NY, I frequented the Jersey Shore when I was younger, until I couldn't take the traffic anymore and found other beach options. The program coined some funny, memorable sayings that caught on with people: "Cab's here"; "gtl, baby. Gym. Tan. Laundry"; and "This is the shirt before the shirt."

When one of the young Jersey-ites was getting dressed for the early part of the evening, like happy hour at the house, they would wear the first shirt; but later when they were leaving to go out for the night, they would put on a new shirt, and so was born, "The shirt before the shirt." I spun that concept into the meeting before the meeting.

When you are so super busy and you have a lot of meetings to be prepped and ready for, set up a meeting before the meeting. Angry parent coming in to discuss a disciplinary incident? Budget meeting with the superintendent? Meeting with the local grocery store to plan a healthy initiative program for the school? Hold a meeting before the meeting with a smaller, closer group, so you can get ready and plan for anything that might come out of the next meeting. Pull your research and all pertinent information together.

We all want to be great communicators with a confident, commanding presence when we are running a meeting. Be prepared and have all the info at your fingertips. Use the meeting before the meeting.

98. Get coffee at meetings.

Teachers and school staff love coffee. They love good coffee, and they really love free coffee. Must be something about working at a school with kids—those early mornings can be rough. Whether you set it up yourself, ask a secretary to help you, or have your café staff help, get coffee for meetings. People like it. Make it happen.

7

Be Careful About Time Management to Optimize Efficiency

99. Use the line, "I need some think-time on that."

People are constantly coming at you; many times without even a greeting or hello. It is all about their request or need and your answer immediately . . . but you are driving your bus. You are sailing your ship. Do not let people grab the wheel while you're driving.

If you are in the middle of something in the hall or the café, tell them they need to wait a moment. If they ask you something that you are not sure of instantly, tell them, "I need some think-time on that." Have your notepad with you and write down their request or concern. I also tell them, "If I miss getting back to you, follow up with me in two or three days and say, 'Hey Mr. Principal, did you have a chance to think about what we talked about last week?'" You do not have to answer people when they are ready. You answer people when you are ready.

100. It is a marathon, not a sprint.

Have you ever run or walked a marathon or long race? Taken a long drive? Committed to an all-day hike? This is a journey you are on, this principal gig. You have to give it some time. You have to give yourself some time.

You are not going to change things overnight. You can start making changes, but it takes a while for "things" to change, so you have to be patient (which was never a strong point of mine). Be patient with people and programs. Think of it as if you are planting a garden. You have to get the seeds, prep the soil, make sure the zone and sunlight conditions are right, water, water, water, mulch, and then wait, wait, wait. You have to watch out for animals, bugs, and other critters getting at your plants. You have to support the plants when they start to grow with braces and wraps. If it is going to be freezing at night, you have to cover your plants. There is a lot you have to do, and in the short term it can seem like tons of effort for minimal reward. But, if you do these things slowly and get them right, with consistent love and care, you will grow a beautiful, bountiful garden with fruit, vegetables, and flowers that keeps giving back to you season after season, year after year.

Cultivating and managing grade school education is a fairly similar process. Many variables can affect the journey: people's health, family relationships, addiction, death, retirements, accidents, egos, politics, and so on. So remember that this is a marathon, not a sprint. Be patient with people and programs. Keep focused on the long-term prize of helping to shape a generation or two with love.

101. Have people make appointments to see you—you are not an emergency room.

This is where a good secretary can really help you. You need to determine what is an emergency and what is not. Most things that come up are not, so have people make appointments to see you. This will slow people down, and it will stop so many things coming at you. You are not a roadside stand that people can just stop at any time they want. You can't just barge into your doctor's office and demand to see the doctor. It is the same deal with you. You are in charge of your schedule and your time is precious, so guard it and have people make appointments to see you.

102. Build in time to breathe.

Build in some time to get out of your office during the day. Step into classes, the café, visit the schoolyard, and so on. I don't take a lunch hour, but I do like to have some free time during the day to be out and about. You can accomplish a lot by seeing people on the go, so leave some room between appointments. Don't schedule everything back to back.

Sometimes when I need a breath, I leave fifteen minutes early for a meeting at the district office (DO). There is a little riverfront beach right near the DO. I like to go there and watch the river for a few minutes. I can open the windows, look out on the water, and take in the quiet. It's peaceful and relaxing, a departure from the nonstop pace in school.

If I do not build time into my schedule, I do not have time to do this for myself. Make it part of your timeline each day, just a few minutes you can spend in a quiet place, preferably outside with fresh air. Your health, your mind-set, and your workday will all be better for it.

103. Be on time for meetings.

Your time is valuable. Honor other people's time as well and be on time for meetings. The only thing better than being prompt is to be early. I am a ten to fifteen minutes early type myself, but at the very least make sure you are on time. This is important.

When you are on time, looking prepared and ready, focused on whatever is in front of you, you are a winner. If you are hustling in late, holding a coffee cup, frazzled and distracted, everyone at the table is thinking to themselves, Really, late again? Aaaaaaand they had time to get a cup of coffee, but couldn't be on time for the meeting?

Set your schedule and make sure you leave plenty of time to get there. Sure, things are going to pop up, but you adjust. Leave time to stop and use the restroom, get that coffee, make extra copies, whatever you need to do. If you are someone who needs an extra push, have your secretary help you. Set your cell phone alarm to go off ten minutes before it's time to walk out the door, so you can wrap up last-minute items and get going. This is not a difficult one, and it is okay if you need a little help. Make it happen.

104. If you are going to be late, have your secretary call and let them know you are running late.

Call. It is so simple, and the least you can do. Let them know that you are late. If something legit happened, inform them. If you're just stuck and running late, do not make up some excuse. Wherever you are going, have your secretary call or call from your cell to inform anyone waiting for you that you are on your way and running behind.

8

Make Time and Pay Attention to Personal Health and Well-Being

105. Get comfortable shoes and wear them.

Along the lines of dressing the part, you need good shoes—comfortable footwear that is functional in the school setting. Your feet and your shoes get beat up at school; you are on your feet a lot—up and down the halls, in and out of classes, visiting the café, you're movin' baby, so get shoes that will be kind to your feet. I recently switched my daily wear to black sneaks. I'm going with the dress sneaker look, and it works for me. You do what works for you, but balance looks with making sure your feet are taken care of. Get shoes that are sturdy and comfortable.

106. Balance your family life and your work life.

You are a son/daughter, husband/wife, and dad/mom first, then a principal. Keep it in that order. I remember before taking the job having a serious, important conversation with my wife about her role in all of this, and how we were going to make it all work. We currently have three children, and we've been married for sixteen years. Even writing this book, Jennifer is behind me 100%. We discuss everything before big decisions are made.

The only way to make it all work is either being on your own or being able to rely on your partner. It is a constant juggling act to balance everything you care about with everyone you are committed to and responsible for. I am not perfect, but I do my best. My family knows they mean the world to me. Last Christmas we celebrated with the family, and then just my wife and I zipped away for a few days at the beach. I was able to catch a break from work, catch my breath, write some of this book, and most importantly, reconnect with my wife.

It is always busy at school; it is easy to come home filled up with your day and all the things swirling around in your mind; but it is supremely important to prioritize your time and devote attention to your family. I have heard from many people many times that "children only have one childhood, so make it wonderful for them." And Dr. Gilbert often says, "Be where your feet are!" The job is important, but family comes first. Make the time, make it happen.

107. Include your family in school events.

You are away from home a lot—at events, night meetings, concerts, games, plays, parent conferences, and so on. When possible, include your family at school events. Let people see that you are human: a father, mother, husband or wife, a son or daughter, a brother or sister. Connect your work family with your home family. Be cautious to maintain privacy for your spouse and children, but bring work and family together whenever there is a picnic, concert, or fun event that lets you be present for everyone at the same time.

108. Eat early and often during the day, and drink plenty of water.

Buckle up. I'm telling you, get ready. In order to do this, you have to eat well and stay hydrated. The job is hard enough on its own, let alone if you do not feel well. This sounds so simple, yet most people do not think about it.

Right now, do you bring your lunch to school? Do you always have a bottle of water on your desk? Have you drunk eight glasses of water today? The answer is most likely no. You've probably had two or more cups of coffee, a soda, and maybe a 5-hour energy boost drink. That may work for a day or two, but if you want to be great in the long run, you have to take care of yourself. Rest, healthy food, and plenty of water; water is your friend. I am a fan of the cup with a straw and triple lemon. I fell in love with the taste and believe the vitamin C in the lemon keeps me healthy. Don't leave meals and snacks to chance if you want to feel your best. I recommend bringing meals or buying them before school to have them ready. Eat small meals and nutritious snacks every two to three hours, and drink close to eight cups of water a day. You are tracking and assessing data on everything else, but are you watching what you eat and drink every day? Start doing it. You'll feel better, and hopefully you'll shoot me a note thanking me. This tip can literally save your life. Drink up!

109. My man Dr. Gilbert challenged me to the Seven C's.

In line with eating small meals more often and drinking water, I also challenge you to give up the Seven C's: Chips, Cola, Chocolate, Candy, Cake, Cookies. Whaaaaaaat? Really? Are you kidding? I was liking this book until I just read that. Is that what you're thinking? Was that your reaction? Wait. That is only six C's . . . the seventh is Complaining. Give it up.

I gave these Seven C's up from Memorial Day to Labor Day, and then again from Thanksgiving to New Years. Man, what a difference. It made me realize the sugar I was eating when I pretty much cut out all the sugar. I couldn't believe it. It's good to put some limits on yourself. You will look better, feel better physically, and feel proud knowing you had the discipline to give up all that junk. Honestly, since I gave up the Seven C's I haven't wanted to eat those things anymore. Good thing the list is C's and not P's. If it were pizza we were talking about, we'd be fighting!!

110. Do something outside of school to counteract the stress.

What is that thing in your life that gets you going inside, besides work or your family? Do it. Do it often and do it for you. For me it is officiating college basketball. I've been refereeing college games at the division one level since 2005, and I love it! My family, my faith, my job, and officiating are the things that keep me sane and grounded, in that order. I work hard to keep them in that order.

Refereeing is something that I have a great passion for. The sweat in the arenas, the energy of the game, the athletes, and the fans all energize me. The game gives me great focus and concentration. It allows me to apply my knowledge of the rules to help ensure a fair contest. Pretty similar to my job as principal, right? Hard work, constantly on the go, enforcing the rules, communicating with coaches and players.

Some people ask me how I deal with the stress of being a high school principal and also a college referee. It's simple—they cancel each other out. When I am in school and engaged with my staff and students, I'm not thinking about the crazy coach who lost his mind the night before, or the tough play in the last three seconds that I called a foul on. I can't think about those things in school, because during the day I have a job to do, and in that moment I've moved on to what's in front of me.

The same is true in the reverse. Let's say I leave school at 4:00 p.m. and drive two hours to another school for a game. I unwind in the car, listening to music, speak with friends, or listen to books on my phone. I then get to the gym, get ready and focused for the task at hand—the game in that moment. I mentally put aside the child who told me to "F&^% off " during the day, and the teacher who was late to school again, or a failed budget at school. . . . For two hours prior to the game and a couple of hours during the game, my mind is off school and the worries of being principal. Balance.

What is the best source of balance for you? Not sure? Let's make a list. Go ahead. What do you enjoy doing outside of your job and your family or relationship obligations?

_____

_____

_____

_____

_____

_____

_____

Is it painting? Running marathons? Cooking? Weight lifting? Woodworking? Hiking? Photography? Charity work? Gardening? Whatever it is, go for it. You need some form of release that will take you out of the grind each day. Find a way to absorb enjoyment and satisfaction from other activities. You will return to the office refreshed and ready to get back at it. Take time for you. Make it happen.

111. Be careful about how you cope with and manage stress.

Stress is a killer. It can eat at some people, and if you are not careful, you could carelessly turn to drugs or alcohol to "ease the pain." I am not here to lecture you, but I can hear my father in my ear, cautioning me how easy it is for people to become addicts.

I'll keep this wisdom point short. Do not let drugs or alcohol abuse become part of your personal life or creep into your professional life. You could lose everything if you allow this to happen. Be strong, stay healthy, and be aware that drugs and/ or alcohol can sneak up on you. Don't let that be you!

112. Read, read, read.

How the heck are you going to find time to do this too? He just told me to balance time with my family, and now he tells me to read?!? Reading is important because it will help you stay current on what's happening in the world. To be a good leader you need to be alert, curious, always seeking a fresh perspective, open to new ideas (like you reading this book right now). Whether it is ten minutes before a school board meeting or on a lazy Sunday afternoon, make time to read and keep current on what's happening in the field of education.

113. FEAR: False Evidence Appearing Real

When there is a lack of trust, everything seems to be against you. Coincidence, or is there some truth to what occurred? My advice: Don't waste time speculating. Stick with hard facts. If something negative is happening against you behind closed doors, or you do not have evidence to support your claims, focus on things you have control over. Stick with what you can manage.

Do not believe everything you hear and do not chase down rumors. Do not read public/anonymous blogs because that will chew you up inside. If there is an issue with someone and they are doing something that is bothering or upsetting you, meet that person face-to-face and address the situation.

Example: You write up a teacher who's been late to work multiple times. The next day that person parks next to you. When you leave work, you find a ding in your door on the side where that person was parked. Coincidence? Did they bang your door on purpose? Did they bang it accidently, or did they not bang it at all, and something or someone not related to that person did it? You'll get yourself in more hot water trying to chase that down than letting it go. A quick check of security cameras doesn't hurt, but you accusing someone who was mad at you because you wrote them up for being late can potentially land you in trouble. Don't let fear eat at you. When you know something, you'll know it.

114. Be careful about social media—personal and school.

My wife and I decided early to skip getting involved with Facebook. Too many people reaching out to ex-girlfriends and boyfriends, old flames, and people from the past. We just never did it. That was in the '90s. While we are still happy with our personal decision, social media has turned into a massive communication superhighway that people from all walks of life use to connect with others for personal and business reasons. As principal, whether you are a beginning user or someone with ten different profiles on every app, be extremely mindful of the content you share. What you post or tweet and comment on, the images you share, all say a lot about you.

Do you want pictures of you drinking alcohol and smoking a cigar at a family wedding to be viewed by a potential employer? Do you want angry, political agenda commentary featured on your personal dialogues? Are you leaving yourself wide open to Internet trolls who spew nonsense jargon and stir up trouble? People are watching everything you do, don't ever doubt it, so keep all social media activity professional, inspiring, and positive.

In the course of writing this book I have been learning to navigate the world of social media, including best ways to connect with others. I'm taking it slow and will manage my content so I know exactly what's being shared in my name. Like anything else, it is one step at a time.

115. Relieve stress during the school day, to stay calm and able to keep up.

Here are two simple things you can do to de-stress while in school, when you can't break away or get outside.

Breathe. Yes, deep, full pattern breaths. Take two minutes in your office before jetting into the hallway or off to your next meeting with that confrontational parent. Start with a deep inhale, like you are going to be underwater for a while. Fill your lungs and hold it for a second or two, then let it out slowly. Round your lips like you are drinking from a straw and let each breath out evenly. It could take twenty to twenty-five seconds to let the breath out completely, and then push out the last bit for a complete exhale, lungs empty. This will instantly calm you. Repeat two or three times and you will feel more relaxed and at ease.

Mini-meditation: 30 seconds, 60 seconds, 120 seconds. Whatever you are comfortable doing. You do not have to chant the infamous Ohmmmmmmm. You can do it simply in two phases. First, envision a place of peace. In Tip 116, you will learn to find your Old Blue Chair, either the ocean where you like to walk, or your hammock in the yard, or a favorite vacation spot. Close your eyes and see yourself there. Take deep breaths and sink into the moment. The second phase of mini-meditation is to practice repeating a mantra or phrase that rings true to you. Repeat it slowly, out loud (obviously not in front of others) or quietly to yourself.

I recognize this may seem strange to some of you, but trust me, I have found that these techniques work for me when I practice them. Dr. Gilbert shared these easy steps with me, and they have greatly improved my life. It was not in my nature to slow down, pause, and take a deep, healing breath in the middle of the day. Being from a big, busy family in Staten Island, I have always been on the go. I grew up in the belief that the faster you move, the faster you get ahead; but as I've gotten older, I have realized the importance of slowing down, taking a breath, and making some time to just be.

116. Find your "Old Blue Chair."

I'm a Kenny Chesney fan. How an Italian from Staten Island became a country music fan is a story for another book, but I love Kenny's music. I enjoy his showmanship, his concerts, and his free spirit. I'm often tightly wound up, and sometimes listening to Kenny Chesney helps me loosen up and relax: no shoes, no shirt, no problems. His fans refer to themselves as No Shoes Nation—a way to claim being carefree, knowing how to kick back and let loose. His songs bring me to a stress-free place of peace and calm. One in particular is the song called: "Old Blue Chair" (www.lyrics.com/lyric/7477409/Old+Blue+Chair).

So, where is your Blue Chair? Take five minutes and give it some thought. Write down three places that take you away, give you an escape, a sense of peace and calm, a location where everything feels right in the world. What makes you consider these three places your Old Blue Chair? What feelings wash over you when you think of being there?

_____

What can you do each day to get to your Old Blue Chair? Write down three ways to ensure you get there more often, on a regular basis, whenever you need to go.

1. _____
2. _____
3. _____

I have a few Old Blue Chairs; not literally, but figuratively. One is walking on the beach with my wife—the sounds of rolling waves, salt on my lips, and the warmth of the sun all add up to a cozy, familiar, comfortable space.

Another Old Blue Chair comparison is walking alone with my dog, Baxter. Sometimes I can steal early time on a weekend, before everyone else wakes up, or sometimes right before dinner. I love being with Baxter. He's loyal, always ready to go out with me, can certainly keep up, never complains, and he's a really good listener! Truly, man's best friend.

My best Old Blue Chair is actually a bench in front of my house. Not just any ol' bench, either. It is a very special bench. We made it in honor of my dad when he passed away. My father loved parks, loved to take walks, and loved to rest on park benches, so what better way to honor him than to make a bench in his memory?

At first we placed Dad's bench in a green space near our home in Staten Island, with a plaque on it that reads:

"In memory of "Mr. Joe" Marotta A lifelong friend of this community. Please help keep it beautiful."

But after a couple of months the NYC parks department made us remove it, because it was an unauthorized, unofficial bench. Mom ponied up the $5,000 to get a real one, but what were we going to do with the one we built together for my dad? I grabbed it, hauled it to my own home, and put it right in front of the house.

Now the bench sits in front where I can see the yard with my children playing, see the street with neighbors and friends passing by, see the house with the sun setting behind it. It is the viewing area for backyard family whiffle ball games. I can sit calmly and relaxed on that bench. I think of my dad and the great times I had growing up. It's my spot. I love it. I like to sit on that bench out front with family and friends to talk, share stories, have snacks, and as my family likes to say, see "what's

IN MEMORY OF "Mr. Joe" Marotta
A lifelong friend of this community.
Please keep it beautiful!

FIGURE 8.1

up." We've hung some of my dad's trinkets there, and that is my Old Blue Chair.

My dad comes up multiple times in this book because I really learned so many lessons from him and my mom, Dorothy. Thanks to my wonderful parents, thanks to Kenny Chesney, and thanks to my own family for all the good times we've shared around the Old Blue Chair.

I'd love for you to watch my father's video of his last marathon. It was filmed in 2008 and you can find it at www.youtube.com/watch?v=hC145Ob0U7E or type in youtube joemarotta marathon. I enjoy sharing his stories and parts of my life with him. This video is a great tribute to him, and I am so thankful to have it with us forever. Shout-out to Ahmed El-Farram for his great film work and friendship.

FIGURE 8.2

FIGURE 8.3

FIGURE 8.4

117. It's not personal.

Letting a veteran teacher know that they had a poor lesson. Writing up a great teacher who is constantly late. Reprimanding an instructor who cursed at a student. Telling a teacher with whom you are friendly that they are not getting the courses they wanted to teach because you need them somewhere else. These situations are going to confront you. Remember that it's not personal.

Education is business, and as company leader you have to make decisions that are best for the school and your students. Assure the adults it is not personal. You can tell people this each and every time you are forced to have these conversations or experiences. Remind anyone at any time that you are making decisions based on what is best for the students and school, because as principal you are the one who has to consider everything and do what's right.

When someone doesn't answer an e-mail from you, doesn't implement a technique you've been asking for in their classroom, or is continually late for work, it (most times) is not personal against you—they just haven't done it or are unable to do it. It isn't because of you. Although sometimes fear (False Evidence Appearing Real) creeps into your mind that the person is intentionally doing _____, I can assure you, it's not personal. Remind yourself and you will get less angry, feel less frustrated, and be able to address issues easily because you can face each challenge objectively. Whether an error in judgment, a mistake, or an oversight, consider it, address it, and move on to the next thing.

9

Transform Setbacks Into Comebacks

118. Don't be afraid to fail.

You will be judged on the amount of times you succeed, not the number of times you fail. It took me many years to achieve this mind-set. I wanted to be perfect: in my marriage, my principal-ship, and in my work as a basketball official. I was pressing too hard to make it all exactly right, and I have learned that I can strive for perfection, but I will settle for excellence.

Think about a baseball player. If they are right three out of ten times, they are an All-Star. Think about how often you are striving to be right or correct, to make your ideas and programs work. You are not going to be perfect every time, so do not be afraid to fail. Did you know that Michael Jordan is in the top ten in missed field goals in the NBA? Really! Did you know that? That means he missed a hell of a lot of shots; 12,345 to be exact. That's not what people focus on, though. It is the number of times you succeed that people remember, so take every shot and hope for the best.

119. Rely on the five SW's for help:

Sometimes it **W**ill,
Sometimes it **W**on't,
So **W**hat,
There's always **S**omeone **W**aiting, and
Stick **W**ith it.

120. Admit mistakes. Adopt the mantra—admit it, fix it, and move on. Don't be afraid to change course if you put something out there that doesn't work.

You will make some mistakes along the way. You might make many. Don't be afraid to say, "Okay, this did not work out like I envisioned," or "This does not look like I wanted it to, and I need to make a change." You will make all sorts of decisions in a lot of areas; they are not all going to be the best ones, so you have to be prepared to back up the train if it isn't working out.

I know you want to be perfect. I know you want to show strength and fortitude as a leader. I know you probably have some bravado in you (you need to, in order to be principal), but it is okay to be human, and important to accept making a mistake once in a while. You go right on ahead and keep reaching for the moon—if you miss, you'll still be among the stars.

121. Accept that not all of your ideas are immediate hits with everyone.

Not everyone is going to love your ideas. There are some people who do not like a program, a schedule change, or a new computer software, just because it was your idea. Get used to this and don't take it personally.

One of the first projects I took on at my school was adding to the dozen or so pennants hanging in the café. My idea was to have all of our teaching staff get pennants from the college or university they attended, and we would hang them in the lunch café. I thought it was a great idea that the staff and students would love. Well, people did like it, but it was like pulling teeth to get people to participate. Predictably, some teachers got their pennant right away; others needed constant reminding, and there were a handful who flat-out were not going to get their pennant. I couldn't believe it. Why would they not participate? After pulling out the little hair I had left, I learned that not everyone will like your ideas, and you can't always get everyone to participate in what you are trying to do!

Some projects and ideas will work out well with lots of enthusiasm, and others will fizzle out or not be quite what you imagined. It's okay. You do what you can, and keep moving forward.

122. The only people that like change are babies with dirty diapers.

Most people don't like change. "Why are you coming in here and trying to change things? We're doing just fine . . . Don't try to reinvent the wheel . . . This is the way I learned and it has worked for thirty years . . . Don't tell me what to do . . . You are taking away my teaching autonomy. . . ." Sound familiar? You are going to hear all of these and more.

No one likes change. It's a weird thing. People just don't do well with it. They get a little nervous, agitated, and question or doubt the reasons behind what you are trying to do. They've seen leaders come and go, education fads come and go, different curricula come and go. The only things that remain are the teachers and staff, so leave them be, right? Not exactly.

You have to be smart and patient with the changes you want to make. Explore every scenario with pros and cons. Invite your advisors to weigh in and say what they think. I talk about the Kitchen Cabinet (see Tip 35), bouncing new ideas off of them prior to introducing changes to the whole staff. It's a good idea to also meet with some of your biggest dissenters. They might offer some good points that you haven't considered.

My friend, a respected veteran teacher is a superstar science teacher at our school. Jim cautioned me against having only "yes sir" people in my ear. He advised me to listen to all parties, even or especially those who typically disagree with new procedures. They can offer good insight. While some pushback may be plain old resistance, there may also be legitimate contract violations or personnel concerns, and those you need to know about. Remember, you are not an expert on the contract or past practice history, so hearing from some of your people can only help you in your efforts to kick-start a new idea.

Collect a variety of viewpoints; imagine every "what if." This is powerful research prior to moving forward, so you know what to expect. There will always be naysayers and doubters; but once you think through all the circumstances and potential risks vs. desired results, develop a plan and stand by it. Believe in yourself, communicate clearly, make information regarding the change easy to find and understand. Listen when people have questions. Follow everything in this book to multiply your chances of a smooth and successful transition every time.

123. Excellence takes extra effort, not standard effort.

Do more than is expected. Do you really want to be great? Sincerely, a great principal? I'll give you the straight-up answer. You can do it! You just have to put the work in.

Look at the word extraordinary. When it isn't enough to be ordinary, you have to do more, go beyond, exceed to excel. It is easy to be average, go into cruise control and continue the things you've been doing; or you can make the commitment to do more, more than is expected of you. Get people's attention. Implement change. Make a difference. This will invigorate you and elevate you to the next level. Make it happen!

124. A setback is a setup for a comeback . . . not the end of the road, a bend in the road.

You will stumble. You will make some mistakes and wrong decisions. My buddy, Dr. Gilbert, shared this with me and it rings true when you misstep: "A setback is a setup for a comeback."

We learned when we were kids that it's not falling off the horse that is the problem; it's getting back on and going again. When you're bumped, bruised, and possibly embarrassed or humiliated, what are you going to do?

You will learn and get better. You will do it again. You will take a deep breath, take stock of the lessons in front of you, and improve with every experience. Don't take each mistake as the end of the world; use each crisis, milestone, and/or encounter to grow.

There are certain grave mistakes like not doing required teacher observations or losing your cool and cursing out a school board member. You might not recover easily from these types of incidents, and if these things are happening, there is a bigger problem. What I'm talking about when I say "setback" is having a bad faculty meeting, or not handling a discipline incident the best way it could be handled, or missing an appointment with someone, not responding to important e-mail, and so on.

Trust me, there are many opportunities to make mistakes or fall short on any given day. In my first year as principal I had several grievances filed against me! Some were frivolous, but others were real mistakes I made. I acknowledged them, fixed them, and made sure they did not happen again. I had to learn to do better, and I did.

10

Handling Difficult Situations

125. What did you do when you found out what you did?

This goes hand in hand with the headline test (tip #14), because if you did wind up in the headlines, on social media, or different social group pages, then you are always judged on this: What did you do when you found out what you did? If you do this long enough, you will get called on the carpet somewhere: a hearing, a discipline situation, questioning from your supervisor, an appeal, a grievance, or at the worst, a courtroom or lawyer's office. So, it is not necessarily what has occurred, because a lot of things are out of your control, yet it is: What did you do when you found out what you did?

This reminds me of a story with one of my APs years ago. He is a great school leader who quickly went on to be a successful and impactful principal. It was picture day and there was a new company that we had contracted with. Historically, we had one subject each take their classes down for the student school pictures, all following an organized schedule. Well, something went awry and the information that they had did not match what we had on our schedule. Things quickly got backed up. There were long lines, crowded hallways, and frustrated staff. I was involved in something else to start the day, when my AP called and said, "We have a problem here" and he further explained what was happening. I said just have them get the student photo cards in order quickly, readjust and get back on schedule. He said it is a greater problem than that and the line that still rings in my ears today: "Andrew, this is not a problem that you caused or created, yet if you don't get down here and make a decision, it is going to become your problem and headache." This line, and my AP's fortitude, I always admired and I thanked him afterwards. I quickly postponed the pictures, met with the management of the photo company, hashed out the problem, and rescheduled for another day. I sent my apologies about the issue to the students and parents, as well as the staff whose classes were disrupted. Like most things, it was important to own the problem, not blame the photo company, and adjust. So instead of a lot of headaches and frustration, we just made a change and moved on.

What did you do when you found out what you did? It would not have been the schedule mix up on their end that people complained about (which was the real issue), but that it was set up poorly, and badly managed, and who created this "disaster"? People like to use this term to describe all problems (pet peeve of mine by the way when people overuse that word) and that would come back on me, the principal. Remember, you're the captain of the ship, so while this was a minor issue with a pretty simple solution, it is not always that easy. Yet, if you make smart decisions, pause, get opinions (when you can), and can defend your decisions when you get called on the carpet, you will be fine.

126. Sometimes it's just best to ignore.

Along with this point of showing strength and confidence, sometimes the best confidence is just to ignore a situation. I am, most times, a man of action, and I value the importance of taking action to improve a situation. It is not in my nature really to just leave something be or let it go. I feel a need to respond and take action with what's happening. This, I have learned, might not always be best.

Unfortunately, as a public figure in schools, people have the right to make public comments about you, voice their opinions about you, and do this in a variety of ways. If you have been doing this a while, this most likely has happened to you: a parent at a public meeting makes a very negative comment about you; someone puts out an e-mail to "all" voicing their opinion about you that touches the line of sarcasm and disrespect; someone puts up a sign with some hurtful words about you. What can you do? What should you do?

As I stated earlier, my first reaction is to respond with strength and defend myself. If someone makes false statements about you or derogatory statements about you or your family, I believe you absolutely should respond and defend your name. If someone offers their opinion of you and/or a decision you made and they do this in an unfavorable or sarcastic manner, sometimes the best course of action is to just ignore them. While this could be bothersome, responding to it may only fuel their fire or prompt the person to act again. Maybe their comment or action will just fade away in a day or two, and you and your true character will move on with your head held high. Those who really know you know your character and will defend you without you having to take any action.

These situations can be tough sometimes, yet so are you. Sometimes, it is best to just ignore. This is an example of showing strength and confidence. Smile, zip your lip, clench that jaw, and move on. It is not what you are going through, it is where you are going to. #KeepRollin #SurviveThrive

127. Be a trauma-informed educator.

In summer of 2019, my district Port Jervis (NY) Schools, under the leadership of our Superintendents, brought our administrative team the opportunity to view and discuss the film *Resilience*. This documentary explores ACES (Adverse Childhood Experiences)

and child trauma and what it can do to children and their families. This really opened my eyes to what some of our children may be going through and the challenges their home lives can present. Viewing this film with my colleagues reminded us to lead with empathy and remember the difficulties many children, families, and staff may be burdened with.

If you have not taken the ACES test, I challenge you to do so. It asks you deep questions about your upbringing and how some of these experiences may have adversely affected you (thus the name of the test: Adverse Childhood Experiences). While I am extremely grateful for the upbringing that my parents gave me, and love them tremendously, I felt guilty that I had a score of 0. I had not been affected negatively by any of the challenges in that test. I realized how blessed and fortunate I am that my parents did such an amazing job raising me and my siblings. This is not the case for everyone and we as educational leaders need to be mindful of this.

I also recommend watching "Under the Surface." This short video found here is another helpful reminder of what people are going through—not only your students, but also your staff at your schools. Again, now more than ever, we need to be trauma-informed educators and leaders and model empathy for those we serve. I recommend showing both of these, the *Resilience* film and "Under the Surface" video at a staff conference day. You will be glad you did.

128. Any injured students, reach out.

Unfortunately, kids get hurt all the time in school: PE class, sporting events, or even at a seemingly innocuous activity. We had a student get hurt at the egg toss event during spirit week! It wasn't even an arm or shoulder, it was a knee!

Often, a student gets injured, heads off to receive medical care, and then life moves on. The next day of school rolls around and you're off again working on all the things you are doing. Sometimes, we forget about that kid and his family. We don't know if that child was up all night in surgery. We don't know about their health. How are mom and dad? If a kid gets injured, it is always a great practice to call later that night and again after a day or two. It shows you care. It shows that you are dialed in, and it follows up on the #1 tip in this book: Treat every kid as if they are your kid. The parents and student will be so thankful that you reached out and took the time to check on that kid. Trust me on this one. The well-being of a child is of the utmost concern to all who know and love that child. So be in the mix right away by calling that night (yes, that night) and again in a day or two. When possible, a visit to the hospital is even better. Yes, this takes more of your time, yet this goes a tremendously long way.

11

How to Be a Connected Leader

129. Using Twitter as a Principal.

After writing this book this first time around, I learned about Twitter and the power of using Twitter (@andrewmarotta21, #survivethrive) as a school leader. Since the first release in 2017, I have connected with so many like-minded leaders and found new, innovative ideas. Read a cool book? You can easily find the author on Twitter and connect with that person. It has made my world as a principal so much smaller and more friendly because I have been able to reach out and share with others who are striving for many of the same things I am. Twitter is a place where you can connect, share, learn, grow, question, reflect, and so on. You can also develop your #PLN (Personal Learning Network): your team of educators and leaders who support you and help you along the way. You don't need to be certified, or purchase anything, and there is no need to make appointments. Your #PLN is always there and always willing to help. Want to ask a question? Ask your #PLN. Want to just listen, learn, and not publish content? You can do that, too. However you want to use it, Twitter is a great tool for you to progressively grow as a school leader.

The great Todd Whitaker (@ToddWhitaker) said that if you are not on Twitter as an educator, then you are falling behind. If you are on Twitter, then keep rolling. If you're not, then get going. If you want to reach out, then I'd love to help you. Contact me at: @andrewmarotta21.

130. Twitter use expanded: Twitter chats.

When the internet first got rolling, and I began to use it in my teens, I always heard about these #chatrooms. They were where creeps went and tried to lure people in to do bad things (not totally true, but I was scared early on to stay out of them.) So when I heard about Twitter chats, I had a negative vibe about them. I stayed away from them and did not participate. Then I made some friends on Twitter from the Massachusetts School Administrators Association (@MSAA_33). Marty Geoghegan (@MGeoghegan) invited me to lead a chat. I told him that I had never done one and didn't know how it worked. He told me that it was no problem, and he handled it all. I buckled up, did a 30-minute chat, and loved it. I describe it like the Millenium Falcon going from regular flying to light speed. Being part of a vibrant Twitter chat is an electric, fast-paced explosion of innovation and ideas from educators around the globe. The leader of the chat (could be you one day!) sets the questions and the time. It usually begins with a round of introductions to see who is on the chat. Then there is a lead question Q1and people start popping up answers from around the globe labeled A1, their answers to Q1 (question 1.) This goes on for 4–6, 7, or 8 questions for either 30 or 60 minutes. It is great. Just awesome because you are learning and sharing with so many educators. You want to get better and learn and they are willing to share with you, interact with you, and try new ideas. I highly recommend this. I went from being a new Twitter user to running workshops around the country about how to use Twitter. In my leadership class for new administrators, I make it part of the course to try Twitter, post work on Twitter, and even participate in a chat. My students have connected with so many great educators and authors who have visited the class virtually and through Twitter: Beth Houf, Jay Billy, Todd Whitaker, Dave Burgess, Evan Robb, Kris Fellicello, and Dan Spainhour. So as Han Solo famously said in *Star Wars* many times about jumping to lightspeed, "punch it" and give it a shot! If you run a Twitter chat, tweet at me (@andrewmarotta21) so I can join you one night!

131. Beth's & Jay's Twitter journey.

Through my PLN and presenting, I have been lucky enough to learn and share the stories of Jay Billy (@JayBilly2) and Beth Houf (@BethHouf). Both are amazing educators, terrific authors, loving parents, and tremendous ambassadors for school leaders around the globe. When I close my eyes and think of what great school leaders should look, act, and be like, I think of these two. We are blessed to have so many educators out there now on social media and beyond, yet these individuals have become two of my closest friends. They each have been generous enough to come on my podcast (Education Leadership & Beyond #ELB), talk with my classes, and help promote my work both on Twitter and through their own work. It has really been amazing and I feel very blessed to have developed these relationships with them and so many others.

I felt it important to share their stories, and to hear them both tell about how they were flatlined before getting on Twitter. I'll start with Jay: Jay shares how he heard the great Todd Whitaker at a conference, and Todd shared a challenge to the audience: "If you are not on Twitter, then you are falling behind as a school leader." Jay had used Twitter previously, but really wasn't active with, or seeing the benefit of, it. He opened up his Twitter after the workshop, and followed Todd. He then started following people who Todd was following and began reading their content. He started to feel inspired, retweeting and liking their stuff, they started following him back, and off he went. He really began to see how using Twitter was helping him as a principal, giving him ideas, and inspiring him. Fast forward several years later, after connecting with Dave Burgess, Jay authored *Lead with Culture*, a best-selling educational leadership book through DBC Publishing. He now continues to impact leaders from around the globe and is an amazing presenter, motivator, and true friend to so many.

Watch his story here: https://bit.ly/ELBJBilly

#Bam, the story grows. Jay is at the National Principals Conference in Nashville, TN, years ago and is in line for nachos and wings (who doesn't want nachos and wings at the NPC (@NASSP), and he bumps into Beth Houf. Beth is a principal in Missouri, was burned out, and ready to leave the field of education. She was gassed. She and Jay begin chatting, and he says, "Are you on Twitter?" Beth reponds that she has Twitter but doesn't really use it. Jay replies, "You're not following the right people. Gimmie your phone!" and begins to follow Todd Whitaker, Dave Burgess, Jimmy Casas, George Corus, and so on using

Beth's phone. He says, "Have you heard of *Teach Like a Pirate*?" Beth responds snarkily that she's heard of all of the "teach likes" and was not really interested in hearing about the pirate. She and Jay continued their conversation and he piqued her curiosity. When she got back to her room, she did google Dave Burgess and *Teach Like A Pirate*. Similar to Jay, Beth started using Twitter and experiencing all its benefits. She loved the *Teach Like A Pirate* message, connected with Dave and his wife Shelley, and she wrote an award-winning book with Shelly called *Lead Like A Pirate*. Beth won the NASSP Principal of the year in 2019 and is an awesome speaker, presenter, and principal. She went from feeling ready to leave the field of education to becoming a star.

See her story in my interview with Beth here: https://bit.ly/ELBBHouf

If these two stories don't motivate you to get on Twitter, I'm not sure what will. Yes, there was a lot of effort that both of these professionals put into their work, but Twitter was an important part of their journey.

132. Learn to share through QR codes.

Want to share your work with other leaders, your staff, community members, and so on? Try using QR codes. Want to do quick surveys with students or staff? Want to continue to use technology to assist you in your work? It is a great way to quickly share out a document, a survey, or really any link. People can use their phones, scan the QR code, and get whatever it is that you put in that code to their phones, Google drive, and so on. Simple.

How do you get the QR code?—also very easy. A quick google search of QR code generators will lead you to a few choices. I have used several and used QR Code Monkey for this book. Copy the link of what you want to use, put it in the QR code generator site, and hit enter and presto! You have a QR code with your document that you can now easily share out to others. Copy it and put it in your presentation or wherever it is you are using it. People can access your document quickly by scanning the code with their phones. The best leaders don't hoard their information and resources—they share them and give them away to help others.

133. Power of storytelling: Open your RAS.

The great Dave Burgess in his book *Teach Like A Pirate* talks about opening your RAS: Reticular Activating System. The RAS is the filtering part of your brain that opens up or closes depending on what type of information it is that you are looking for. In his book, Dave references buying a minivan and tells the story of how his family knew nothing about, nor paid any attention to, minivans until this time when they were getting ready to purchase one. To explain this, I'll use the example of RVs. I was not an RV or trailer guy at all. I preferred a Marriott any day. One snow day, when we watched way too much TV, a commercial for Arches National Park in Utah came on. My kids were locked in and begged us to go. My wife and I had wanted to take our family to the national parks out west, and so we started researching the trip: location, travel, RV parks, interstates, and RVs. I had never noticed RVs on the road before. I guess I would just wiz by them in my car and never really paid attention to them. Once I began researching renting them, I saw them everywhere. Each day, when I drove, I saw all different types of RVs all over. I noticed the different styles, lengths, models, and so on. Before long, we made our decision and we were traveling out west in the RV and arrived at Arches National Park, as well as many other parks. We're going on year four of national park trips and have fallen in love with these trips and the time together with our family.

The point: Storytelling and what this can do for you as a school leader. People love stories, especially well told ones. They like funny ones, powerful ones, love stories, heart touching stories and more. There are tons of stories and after doing so many conferences and workshops for school leaders, many ask: "Where do you get the stories?" My answer is always: "I opened my RAS!" They think I am cursing at them and look at me funny, yet I explain that if you just start looking for, listening to, and gathering stories, you'll get them. You'll find them. Even if they are other peoples' stories to start. As long as you credit the person, it's fine. Your audience will still enjoy the stories.

Here are a few tips to get you started on collecting stories:

◆ Call the success hotline and my friend Dr. Rob Gilbert.
◆ Watch TED talks, especially on noneducational topics.
◆ Go to different places that you may not normally: an off-broadway/off-main street play or presentation.
◆ Buy the book *Leading Narratives* by Dan Spainhour and subscribe to his journal: the "Coaching & Leading Journal."
◆ Be ready: I always have my black book in my pocket. When I hear a story, I write it down.
◆ Listen to podcasts and read books.
◆ Go to storytelling workshops. They're out there, including mine!
◆ Talk with your elders: After living a lifetime, they always have great stories.
◆ Just do it: start telling them to anyone who will listen. The more you tell, the better you'll get.

Good luck. I make it a point to start or end almost any meeting with a story. People will forget what you say, yet a great story may stay with them for a lifetime. Open your RAS and start finding the stories! Your stories!

134. Bring a TED Talk to your school.

I visited Goshen (NY) Central School District in the spring of 2019 to watch the TED talk that they set up in their school district. I have loved TED Talks for a long time, and to see one up close and personal was amazing. It was a great, professional production organized and implemented by Jonathan Redeker and Eric Harris. Both are educators in the Goshen School District and were kind enough to share their story with me. If you have never been to a TED Talk, I highly recommend it and kudos to these gentlemen for bringing it to their school district and community. You can learn more about their work on Twitter: @JonRedeker and @eric_harris5.

Here is their TEDxGoshen story:

Incredible things can happen when certain people cross paths at certain times. Thus was the genesis of TEDxGoshen.

We—Jon Redeker and Eric Harris—met in the fall of 2017. It was obvious our educational philosophies were aligned, but more importantly it was clear that we had parallel ambitions regarding how we wanted to carry out that philosophy.

For years, one of the culminating activities of Eric's 10th grade English curriculum was something titled "Sophomore Talks." At the time, Jon had been running something similar with his seniors in Participation in Government called the "Civic Action Project." The tagline for Eric's project was: You may not be able to change the world, but you can change the way we all think about the world. Jon's was: Regular people can make social change. We didn't know it at the time, but TEDxGoshen would later embody these ideals. Then, in May of 2018, we engaged in an e-mail exchange with the subject line: "Time to think big." And we were on our way.

TEDxGoshen is a local, independently organized TEDx event in Goshen, New York. Our mission is to re-create the unique experience found at TED at the local level. At its core, the fundamental goal of the organization is to cultivate "ideas worth spreading." Our aim is to provide a platform where we empower voices in our community to speak to an authentic audience with a global impact. We held our first event on June 4, 2019, and it was a rousing success.

Our "why" was obvious from the start. We believe that our role as educators is to help facilitate personal and authentic learning experiences for students, and we have personally worked with adolescents who have big ideas and world-changing beliefs. It became apparent that we needed to elevate their voices to others. Partnering with the TEDx organization helped give students, alumni, and community members a global voice representing our small town.

We also understood that speakers with profound voices and captivating stories were the heartbeat of this event. Our speakers ranged from 13 to 55 years old and came from a wide array of cultural and socioeconomic backgrounds. One speaker, a high school junior, talked about the importance of being present in a digital age; another speaker, a Goshen community member, discussed the power of giving. An 8th grader shared her struggle with people pleasing while staying true to herself. Another speaker, a Goshen alumnus, communicated her idea of perseverance through her journey to the United States from Israel and later graduating from Cornell. You can watch more of these talks at tedxgoshen.com.

To think we could have succeeded without the help of a strong staff would have been foolish. Besides, we are not narcissists. We have always understood, and even preached the value of building good teams throughout our careers. We are coaches and leaders by nature (Eric coaches varsity basketball and Jon is the instructional technology leader in Goshen), so we understand the value of teamwork. We started as a team of two and quickly realized that we needed to reach out to our larger network to find experts in different areas. As we worked to organize this event, it became apparent that we had incredible talent within our Goshen friends and colleagues. The event would not have been as successful without the support from the incredible team handling creativity, logistics, A/V, stage production, writing, and performance.

One of the most moving moments in our TEDxGoshen experience was when Jack, a junior from Goshen High School, shared his struggle with the stigma of substance abuse as it related to someone in his immediate family. In his talk, Jack opened up his heart to the audience as he pinpointed the way so many of us treat addicts who try valiantly to seek help. Through his personal story, he challenged everyone in the room to be better when it comes to empathizing with those in need of support. Remember, he was 16 years old.

In truth, most of our speakers rose to the occasion and delivered the best renditions of their talks the night of the event. When planning for any performance, you hope people peak during the performance. We were overwhelmed with emotion for those who did. Some of our speakers may have stumbled and struggled with some of their talks, but their recoveries and fight to go on were admirable and—to some extent—symbolized the theme of our event: grit. Some veteran teachers and administrators mentioned to us that this was "the best event" they have seen in education in their 40 years of experience. We thought so too. It was good to hear that our work landed in the community and across the globe with that impact as well.

Our 2019 theme: Goshen, New York finds itself at a metaphorical and literal crossroads. Functioning as the county seat of Orange County, Goshen is a rural town located near the intersection of two major highways. Many people are watching Goshen as it works through the tension as a historical landmark while expanding with new businesses and people. Goshen is the home of the Cradle of the Trotter and celebrates that heritage at the historical track and museum. Noah Webster, founding father of the American educational system and Webster's Dictionary is a celebrated member of Goshen's history. Meanwhile, Goshen School District is developing modern facilities, teaching practices, technologies, and ideas. Goshen is also experiencing corporate growth and investment that is both foreign and challenging to many of the long-time residents. TEDxGoshen will be a forum for members of the entire community, young and old, to expound on what it means to identify with Goshen. Living with tension between preserving historical identities while forming new ones in the community takes a certain amount of "grit," defined by Webster as "unyielding courage in the face of hardship or danger." The Goshen School District mascot is the gladiator, which exemplifies much of the character of living with tension. It is with that in mind that TEDxGoshen will be branded as "Gladiator Grit."

TEDxGoshen 2020: TEDxGoshen was planned for the Spring of 2020, but was put on hold due to the COVID-19 Pandemic. Students had begun submitting video promotions of their proposed talks via FlipGrid, and they have been outstanding.

135. Send birthday cards to all staff.

I got this idea from my friend and mentor, Dr. John Bell. Dr. Bell is an amazing educational leader from Port Jervis, NY who is the Superintendent of Delaware Valley Schools in Milford, PA, where I reside with my family. In addition to sending personal notes of recognition, add birthday cards to the mix. Do a short google survey, get everyone's birthday (everyone: custodians, secretaries, and so on . . . not just teachers), have your secretary address each of them, and put them in order by date. Have your secretary again help you by giving you each card about a week before the person's birthday. You can then fill each one out and write a note of appreciation in the card. Don't just sign your name and say happy birthday. Like most everything in this book: do a little more. Write how much you appreciate them, acknowledge and ask about their family, share how you enjoy _____about them working in the school, and so on. No matter how old we are, people appreciate this. When I started this in the 2019–2020 school year, most of those who I wrote to told me how much they appreciated the card and note. So for a few bucks for the cards and a few minutes of your time, your efforts go a long way in deepening your relationships with the people you work with.

136. Go to all the events?

In the fall of 2018, we had a change of APs, and we hired Justin Karram. Justin moved he and his wife from the Western, NY area to Orange County, NY and dove right into the work in Port Jervis schools. This was his first administrative position and Justin worked very hard. He got to the office early and stayed late and did everything asked of him. What happened after school was really beautiful to watch. As I wrote in the above point about the importance of going to community events, Justin took this to the extreme. He had the perfect situation of living in town, his wife working late, and not having children of his own yet, so Justin decided that he was going to go to ALL the events. I mean all. He made so many connections with students, families, and community members. He began to get invited to the dugout during baseball and softball games, would be able to talk with students the next day about what happened at a certain event, and was also able to handle a lot of "extras" because he was at these events. Instead of a phone call the next morning, Justin may have seen a parent right there at the event and connected face to face right there. The one time he did have to miss a football game because he was at another school-sponsored event, the football team brought a cardboard cutout caricature of Mr. Karram and put it on the bench.

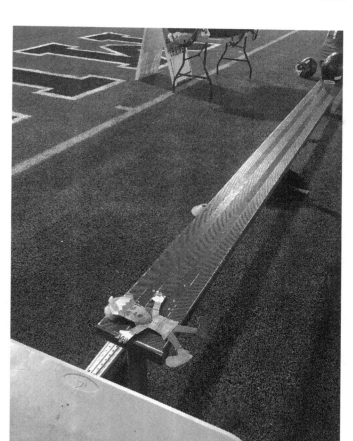

FIGURE 11.1

Because of his commitment to be at all of these events, he found a home in a new community quickly and was able to navigate all the challenges that come with being a new AP just a bit easier. Kudos to Justin for his commitment to going to all of the events. While this may not be possible for everyone (families, commuting, your own wellness, etc.), this young man made this commitment and I am proud of him for it. I could feel that he was #allin when I met him, and he certainly demonstrated it through these actions.

137. Create a workshop and go for it.

If you haven't ever done one yet, create a workshop that you believe in, are passionate about, and get to a conference to present it. Most states have administrative leadership conferences that you can apply to present at. Sessions usually run 60 to 75 minutes. A simple google search of "Call for Proposals" and maybe the state you are looking for a conference in will get you started in the right direction.

So why try doing this? Here are some positives that can come from it:

1. It will energize you to create and share something that helps others.
2. It will strengthen your presentation skills, making you a stronger presenter for your staff and students.
3. You can even run this workshop after school or on a conference day for staff in your district.
4. It will strengthen your knowledge of the subject area that you are discussing.
5. It will connect you with other educators.
6. You will bring positive recognition to yourself and your school.
7. It will boost your confidence in your public speaking and time management. Create a small google form to give after your session and you will get great feedback. Not sure what questions to ask? Reach out to @andrewmarotta21 on Twitter and I will be happy to assist.

After you do this, what will you say when you look back—"I'm glad I did" or "I wish I would have"? Go for it. #thepowerofasingleexperience

138. Two great questions to ask your interview candidates.

I love reading Dan Rockwell's daily blog, "The Leadership Freak." He provides great insight into so many aspects of leadership, and especially the work we do as leaders in education. Here is a great blog from Dan where he shares two questions we should ask when hiring:

TWO INTERVIEW QUESTIONS THAT HELP YOU HIRE THE RIGHT PEOPLE

February 17, 2020

Leaders tell me, "I can't find good people."

What if the talent war is the wrong war? Maybe you're looking in the wrong place and asking the wrong questions.

Success is more about grit than talent.

Dumb people succeed and smart people underperform. Your performance in school has almost nothing to do with your performance at work.

Hire for character:

"Character is, in the long run, the decisive factor in the life of individuals and of nations alike." Theodore Roosevelt

". . . one characteristic emerged as a significant predictor of success. It wasn't social intelligence. It wasn't good looks, physical health, and it wasn't IQ. It was grit." Angela Duckworth

Hire based more on grit than on talent.

Duckworth continues, ". . . in our data, grit is usually unrelated or even inversely related to measures of talent."

Talent and grit are usually inversely related? Really?

If Duckworth is right, highly talented people tend to give up sooner than people with less talent. Will Smith agrees when he preaches the value of hard work over talent.

". . . where I excel is ridiculous, sickening work ethic . . . while the other guy's sleeping, I'm working."

Should you hire dingbats who have grit? Probably not. Thomas NG and Daniel Feldman's research suggest that education matters.

How to hire for character:

Helen Keller said, "Only through experience of trial and suffering can the soul be strengthened, ambition inspired, and success achieved.

Interview question #1.: Tell me about a time when you struggled through adversity. What changed about you?

Interview question #2: Tell me about a time when you worked long and hard to develop a skill. What did you learn about yourself?

139. Attend a Principals' Conference.

In 2019, I attended the National Principals' Conference in Boston, MA. It was off the charts incredible. #impactful #inspiring #PLN connecting I loved it. Is every conference like this? Is each year going to be like this? The answers are no and I hope so. I was blown away by #NASSP and the work they do. They had an amazing lineup of speakers and presenters in a professional venue and with a perfect schedule. I highly recommend you attend the national conference if you are able. I connected with educators from around the country including Alaska (yes, Alaska!) and was able to grow, share, and learn from so many.

Here is just one takeaway: One speaker I was going to see had travel issues and was not able to make it, so I went back a second time to see the great Jimmy Casas (awesome books

Culturize and *Live Your Excellence* @casas_jimmy). While I was not blown away by the title of the workshop, *Best Practices in Hiring,* I was blown away by Jimmy and what he was sharing. In a short time, Jimmy totally flipped my beliefs about hiring and said something that was so impactful to me: "When these candidates are done with me, they are going to be dying to work for my school and me as their leader." And this was all before the interview!

Jimmy shared that he did the following:

- ◆ Called the candidates himself and gave a short mini-interview over the phone.
- ◆ Gave the candidates the first question of the interview: Tell me a little about yourself and why you want to come work in _____s schools.
- ◆ Reserved parking spots for the candidate and gave them his cell in case they had any questions.
- ◆ Set up student greeters who met the candidates outside and walked them in. These students gave a brief tour of the school and made the candidates feel at ease.
- ◆ Offered great flexibility in allowing for different interview times if people couldn't make it. I was of the old school that these were the times of the interviews and if the candidate couldn't make it, too bad.
- ◆ He also shared that he did everything he could to make the candidate feel as comfortable as possible for the interview, and ease any nervousness. He wanted to put them in the best situation possible to succeed, not intensify things and see how they do.

I loved all of these ideas and more and was texting my secretary and APs during the session. We implemented these techniques and strategies immediately and have been doing them ever since. I love them and I loved Jimmy's message. People who interviewed with us raved about the parking reservations, the student tours, and how welcome they felt. It has been a great change for me in mindset and practice and I am ever grateful to Jimmy Casas for his mentorship, leadership, and certainly sharing his hiring practices.

140. Find something positive to say about people at the meeting.

At each meeting, I always like to share a story, find a positive, or celebrate something. This is very important: Find something positive to say about at least one person in the room. If there are going to be ten people in your meeting, sit and reflect for a few minutes, and find something positive to share about someone in the meeting. A few examples:

- ◆ I was in Mrs. Smith's room this morning, and she did the most amazing engagement activity to kick off the lesson. She had all of the students standing up . . .
- ◆ I had a chance to meet Mike's daughter this week. She was just so adorable, and really bright. When I asked her favorite subject, she just lit up and said "recess!"
- ◆ I'm really proud of Tim as he represented our school last week at the county meeting. He presented on being trauma-informed and was just amazing. I received so many compliments about his presentation. Tim would you like to share a little of what you spoke about?
- ◆ I got an e-mail today about Mrs. Lacent from a parent that I wanted to share. She went on to say . . .

These are short amounts of time, don't cost you anything, and get people feeling good about one another. If you begin to do this more and more, it helps add to the culture of positivity in your school, and specifically your meetings. You are modeling for others, and certainly making the person you are speaking of feel good. Make sure you spread it around, even if you have to dig deep to find something about some people. That's okay; seek, and you shall find. Speaking positive breeds positivity.

141. Give audible a try.

Being a busy principal, sometimes it's really hard to make time to read. You are up late, getting ready for your next meeting, finishing up those observations, and so on. I know many times during the school year, when I make plans to read before bed, I shave off that reading time because I just want to do this real quick, or let me take care of that . . . it will only take just a couple of minutes. Before I know it, I'm getting into bed at 10 p.m., and my head hits the pillow and I'm out.

One thing I do to counteract this is listen to books on audible. This is the app through Amazon that you can use to listen to books. Much like the old "books on tape" or a CD. It is really very simple. I listen often in the car, especially when I have a long drive, and I also enjoy listening on long walks. The books take me away from busy thoughts in my brain and allow me to "get away" within the book.

You may say that you enjoy marking up a book: underlining, highlighting, and so on so you can go back to it later. Well, you can do a similar practice on audible. Hear something you like that the author reads? "Clip it," name the clip, and you can save it in a section in the app so you can play it later. I have played multiple clips in faculty meetings and observation reviews with teachers. It can be a useful tool as well as a recreational escape. Give it a try!

142. No applause, no feedback.

So what can you do if you are unable to "bring it"? No, I'm not talking about not being able to muster up the energy during the school day. I'm talking virtually. I am writing these additional learning points during the time of the Covid-19 virus school closures and one of the many changes and things that we, as educators, had to adapt to was receiving little to no feedback on our work. Specifically, on our interactions in our virtual meetings. Unlike in school, after we give a talk to a group of students, or hold a faculty gathering, we can "feel" the room. We can get a vibe of where people are and if we need to adapt how we are doing something, or tweak the message or information. We can bring the energy in those settings, like I wrote about in the previous point, yet with most people muted in virtual meetings, and you sharing your screen often, you cannot see or feel your audience. How can you get a read on what's happening? If they are into what you are doing?

My family and I watched a virtual concert during the Covid-19 shutdown, and while the songs were beautiful, it was eerily weird and awkward with no applause or cheering after the song was completed. No feedback, no nothing? These virtual meetings and presentations can be quite challenging because of this dynamic. Here are few recommendations for you to try:

1. Ask! Stop multiple times during the session and do check ins. You can always pause, and allow for some q&a. As my sister Suzanne Carbonaro (@suzieprof) shared in a virtual training she did, she recommended the "power pause." This allows the audience to jump in and you to gather yourself. It also allows for the content of what you are discussing to sink in a little deeper.

2. Use online participation tools like mentimeter or pad-let. You can share your screen and put a mentimeter up there and ask a few questions. You can take votes, polls, and even ask the question: How are you feeling? I like the word collage feature as well, as it gives you a pretty cool design afterwards. The bigger the word in the collage, the more people wrote it.

3. Do a google survey afterwards so you can get targeted feedback and make improvements for your next session.
4. Try the wheel of names online tool. This is a random name selector that you can ask a question, and then almost in a game show kind of way, select a person to participate. This will help you when there are a lot of people in your meeting or training session.
5. Make sure your content is on point. When you bring strong and meaningful info to the session, people are more likely to be dialed in. Share it via a QR code or link and have pertinent information to the topic you are discussing.
6. Lastly, laugh, tell a great story, and be authentic. Don't be too serious, too long, or too much. Do what you gotta do, and end the session promptly, or maybe even a bit early. Who doesn't like more time? People will enjoy a smile that you helped create. You can enjoy it too, even if you can't see their smile!

143. The Try Method.

After starting the #ELB podcast in 2018, I was able to meet a number of amazing leaders, educators, and coaches. Each episode is like my own personal professional development that I get to share out with others. It was special to interview my brother, Paul Marotta, chemist at the Estee Lauder company on Education Leadership & Beyond #ELB episode 67. Paul and I shared a lot during the conversation and one of my favorite takeaways was asking him about ideas and new products. He shared: "We use the tri method!" So I waited patiently for him to share some mathematical formula, chemical education, or complicated rubric about what the tri method actually was. It is really the try method, and Paul went on to say "We try this, or we try that, until we find something that works. In baseball, if you try and are successful 3 out of 10 times, you are an all-star.

In chemistry, it's one out of 100s and you have done something great!"

1. I am not sure what the success rate on new ideas or trying new things in education is or should be, yet one thing I am sure of is that we shouldn't be afraid of "the try method." Let's try some new things. See what works in our school, in your school, and more things that work for kids. My buddy, Jared Kahmar, principal at HBE Elementary tried two really cool things in his building when he started out as principal that I love: He starts his announcements over the loudspeaker with the NBC tune, ton, tune bell sounds. Everyone loves it and he gets their attention. He also holds "fireside chats" with his students with a nice fire on the big screen behind him, a comfortable chair, a warm mug, and hundreds of little kids on the floor listening to his every word. I "tried" doing my morning announcements years ago with the "Goooooooooooooood Moooooorrrrnnnning Staff and Students . . . . . ." Know where I got that from? Why I "tried" it? Depends on your age if you'll know it, yet it was from Robin Williams in "Goooooooood Moooooorrrrrnnning Vietnaaaaaaaaam." I started doing it and it stuck! Don't be afraid to "try" new things!

12

Focus on the Goal

144. Successful or significant?

I hope you've enjoyed this book. I hope you've found something useful; information and/or wisdom that will help improve your daily function at school. You bought this book for a reason, most likely because you want to be better. Take any tip featured here and make it your own. That is what I did with many of these lessons and anecdotes. I learned them from my family, mentors, and supervisors; picked them up from experiences with parents, teachers, and students. I incorporated them into my work at school and made them my own in my career. I hope you will do the same, and I ask you: Are you trying to be successful, or significant? How do you define these goals? What will be your measure? What makes a successful principal? Is it high test scores, low incident rates, high teacher retention, high graduation rates? In the end, there are many factors that influence your success (and plenty of people happy to measure you along the way).

After doing this for many years, I have learned that yes, we all want to be successful; but the real goal, the real treasure is in being significant—significant in the lives of your students, your staff, and your community. You will make a couple of bucks and maybe receive a few acknowledgments over time, but in becoming a great principal, you have the opportunity to make a significant, positive impact on others; and when you can achieve being significant, I can think of no greater form of success.

I have included two of the most powerful letters I have received from students in my career. These letters melt my heart and certainly make me believe that being significant in the lives of my students really is truly one of the most important things I can do. There are no bonuses in this business, just letters of gratitude like these two from two awesome students. I feel lucky to be their principal and humbled by their words.

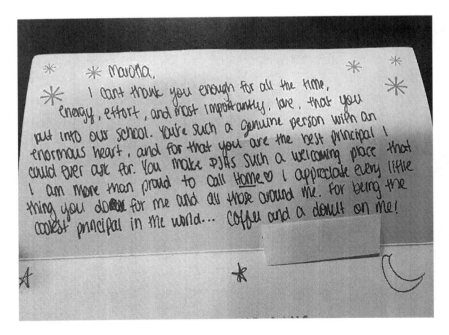

FIGURE 12.1

Mr. Marotta,   6 | 1 | 17

I cannot say thank you
enough for how welcome you've
made me feel ever since 9th grade
when I was the "new kid". You
made Port Jervis High School my
home I will always remember
EVERY WORD to the song "Happy"
thanks to you playing it every
friday of my sophomore year.
Your kindness and willingness to
make me feel at home here in PJ
have been a prime example to me
of what it means to be a leader.
So thank you. I am beyond proud
to attend Port Jervis High School and
I am even more thrilled that I
have 3 more siblings that will be
attending this school. I am so so so
grateful for the lessons I have
learned + morals/values I have
gained through this school.
It doesn't get much better than
this.
Thanks for all the love kindness and
support you have shown me those
past 4 years, I will be forever
grateful!

        Much love

FIGURE 12.2

I sadly attended the wake of my assistant principal's father, Paul Rickard, Sr. Coach Rickard was an outstanding teacher and basketball coach in Orange County, NY for over 30 years. He was an even better person—a husband, father, and grandfather.

In the homily, the priest spoke about the most important part of the tombstone. He said it is the dash. Yes, the dash—the little line between the numbers, because that's where life is lived. As I end this book, I hope it will add to the principal portion of your dash. I hope the wisdom points, tips, and stories as I've shared them help to make your professional, education dash not just successful, but significant. Thank you for investing in this book. I wish you nothing but the best. Go for it with all you've got, and no matter what, don't let them get you down!

Afterword

Making the Most of This Book

Below are some "How To's" on using this book and its contents to the fullest. You can read it, stick it on the shelf, and not make any changes. Things will remain as they are for you, which may be good, or maybe not. Or you can read it, follow these How To's, and implement some of these tips to improve not only your role as a school leader, but also enrich the lives of those around you, the ones we serve: our staff, students, and community. Go for it. Go all in and you will be pleased with your results.

Pick One Thing and Try It

There are so many tips and so many actions for you to try all at once in here. Pick one thing and try it. Try it tomorrow. You don't need training. You don't need permission. You don't need a license. So many of these tips are just practical real things that you can do. You just have to start. Pick the one you like and just start it. Then make it your own. Add to it, tweak it, change it and make it your own.

Give Yourself Time

People and programs take time. If you are trying any of these tips (yes, some are easier than others), give yourself time: time to actually do them, time to think about them, time to make them your own. Be intentional about them: Put them on your schedule, your to-do list, your planner, and get them done. Make the important thing the important thing and get it done. When you look back at the end of your day, your week, your year, or your career, you will be happy you did.

Forgive Yourself

You are going to make mistakes, miss things, and slip up. Don't beat yourself up. There are enough people that may try to do that. You have to be patient with yourself, focused on growth, and forgive yourself when you make mistakes, because you will. I found out early that when I made/make mistakes, I followed this mindset: Admit it, fix it, and move on. Somewhere in there, I also forgave myself. You should too.

Read Some of the Tips With the Person That Will Help You Take Action

Your administrative team, office personnel, parent group, teacher leadership team—bring your people into the mix and share some of the tips that you want to implement. Let them hear your voice, your vision. Let them provide some ideas and join in the collaboration. Sometimes it's your call, sometimes it's a collaboration, and sometimes you let them take the reins, yet bring them into the mix on what it is you are trying to accomplish. People will not break down supports and systems they helped build, so bring them into the mix. This will also help you delegate some of the tips so you can do others.

Come Back to These Tips

Maybe you got away from picking a yearly theme, stopped mailing birthday cards, or stopped getting the pretty flowers for the front of the school. Re-read some of the tips and bring it back. Again, you do not have to ask anyone or get approved, you just have to take action and start doing them again. Come back to the tips again and again. The more you do them, the more regular habits they will become.

Map Out Your Year and Break It Up Into Four Quarters Including a Summertime Work Period

Planning time: this is so important, crucial to your success as a school leader. Whether it is late June, early July, or August, make some time to plan out your year. Go through the book and write down when you will do what tips. Some are a one-time event, some are on-going. For example, if you are going to get coffee at faculty meetings, put it on the calendar 1–2 days before the faculty meeting so you or someone you delegate to can make time to prepare. If you are going to visit other schools, mark it down once per quarter that you are going to do this. Set a goal that you are going to look for at least three takeaways from each building. By the end of your year, you will have twelve new ideas that you may want to start to try. I wouldn't recommend doing them all at once, but at least you will have them to try.

The other important reason for doing this exercise is so you "chunk the year." Meaning, you do not have to face and conquer a whole school year, just one quarter at a time. Do an amazing job to kick off the year and get to that first quarter date. You don't have to complete all twelve months at once, just three at a time. Too big a time to tackle, split it in half and make it five-week chunks. My school uses progress reports and report cards, spaced out five weeks at a time. Get to that new progress report, just five weeks away. Do great things during this time and display tremendous energy. Then you can reset, catch your breath, recharge, and keep going. #Chunkthework

Believe in Yourself

If you are in your first year or two, you might be hesitant about some of these things. Maybe you are afraid of some negative backlash or unsure about how things might be received. So what. Believe in yourself and tell yourself that you can do this.

Try this: Stretch your right hand out in front of you, looking at all five of your fingers. Take your thumb and touch it to your pointer finger and say the word "I." Next take your thumb and touch it to your middle finger. Say the word "can." Next take your thumb and touch it to your ring finger and say "do," and lastly touch it to your pinky and say "this." That's right. You can do this and you have to believe in yourself. If you don't believe in yourself, who else will? Confidence is contagious. Confidence is attractive. Confidence helps you move forward, even if sometimes you have to fake it. I can do this. Yes. You can do this.

Do This Activity With Either Your Administrative Team or Your Secretaries

You each pick 10 tips in the book. Grade yourself on a scale of 1 to 10 on how you are doing those actions or behaviors right now. Then build your action plan on how you are going to implement those tips in your world as a school leader. Set a date two months from now and then re-grade yourself. How did it go? What changes did you see? What actions did you take? Are you happy with the results? If the answer is yes, pick 10 more tips and repeat the process. If you are not happy with the results, repeat it and do it again for two months. The more you repeat these actions, the more these items will become habits. The more they become habits, the more you will naturally do them and they will become part of your routine.

This is an example of the Success Cycle. I reference Dr. Rob Gilbert, sport psychologist from Montclair State University, many times in this book. I learned this from the good Dr. Imagine looking at a clock: At 12 o'clock is the phrase: The more you do something. Next at 3 o'clock is the phrase: The better you get at it.

6 o'clock: The better you feel about it. 9 o'clock: The more you like it. Simply put, the more you do something, the better you will get at it and feel good about doing it, so you will keep doing it. It makes total sense. The success cycle and doing these habits in the book go hand in hand with each other. The more you do these tips and hacks, the more you will continue to do them because you will like the results. It is a true win–win scenario. You will make others feel good and you will feel good in turn.

Good luck. You can do it. I wish you the best.